PASTORAL THEOLOGY

AND THE

MODERN WORLD

BY THE

REV. CLEMENT F. ROGERS, M.A.

PROFESSOR OF PASTORAL THEOLOGY, KING'S COLLEGE
UNIVERSITY OF LONDON
AUTHOR OF 'AN INTRODUCTION TO THE STUDY OF PASTORAL
THEOLOGY', 'CHARITABLE RELIEF'; 'CIRCUMSTANCES OR CHARACTER?'
'PRINCIPLES OF PARISH WORK'

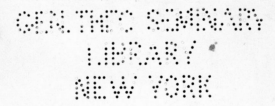
OXFORD UNIVERSITY PRESS

LONDON   EDINBURGH   GLASGOW   NEW YORK
TORONTO   MELBOURNE   CAPE TOWN   BOMBAY
HUMPHREY MILFORD
1920

The scope and mark which we are to aim at is τὸ κοινόν, the public and common good of all; for the easier procurement whereof, our diligence must search out all helps and furtherances of direction which scriptures, councils, fathers, histories, the laws and practices of all churches, the mutual conference of all men's collections and observations may afford; our industry must even anatomize every particle of that body which we are to uphold sound.

HOOKER, *Ecclesiastical Polity*, Dedication to Bk. V, § 10.

Scholars ought to be diligent . . . in the driving of their general school-rules ever to the smallest actions of life: which while they dwell in their books they will never find.

GEORGE HERBERT, *The Countrey Parson.*

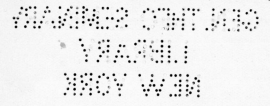

PREFACE

THESE lectures were planned before the war, written during the hard days of the long drawn-out struggle, and are published now that we have won through to our deliverance. The industrial organization of Society has again become a matter that colours all our thoughts, and the Church needs even more than before to adapt her methods to present conditions and to fit herself to cope with the needs of men in the world of to-day. Longer views, and enlarged outlook, efficiency, aims clearly seen and pursued, concentration of purpose to deal with the things that matter most in view of the immense issues at stake ; these are the things for which I plead in the following pages.

Military terms have furnished titles for the last two chapters, but the others might equally well have been named from the part to be played in the Holy War by sustained effort as opposed to mere guerilla warfare (Ch. I), by the organization of an army (Ch. II), by the training of officers (Ch. III), and by the plan of campaign (Ch. IV).

To these lectures I have added some papers dealing with allied subjects. That on Pastoral Theology and Art should have been a chapter in my *Introduction to the Study of Pastoral Theology*, but was, strangely, thought of too late. The others deal with various problems of Church Work suggested by personal experience. I am indebted to the Editors of the *Church*

Quarterly Review, the *Commonwealth*, the *Guardian*, the *Church Times*, and the *Eldermote Review* for permission to reprint them here. I am also under great obligations to the Rev. Prof. Claude Jenkins for many valuable criticisms and suggestions.

One word more. The first chapter may seem to deal with small matters and to be addressed only to the clergy. I believe that little things lead on to big. May I ask lay or impatient readers to turn first to Chapter VI, and they will see the larger ends I have in view.

CLEMENT F. ROGERS.

KING'S COLLEGE HOSTEL,
    VINCENT SQUARE, S.W. 1.
        Jan. 19, 1920.

CONTENTS

CONTENTS

REPRINTED ESSAYS

CHAPTER I

THE SPAN OF WORK

' An inability to stay quiet, an irritable desire to act directly, is one of the most conspicuous failings of mankind.'—WALTER BAGEHOT, *Physics and Politics, Works and Life,* vol. viii, p. 120.

PROGRESS in civilization has been in large part due to increase in man's power to look ahead. The savage lives from day to day, hunting and feasting, and then hunting again. Pastoral and nomadic tribes live from season to season, moving on when pasture is exhausted or water fails with the summer's drought. Agricultural peoples look on from year to year, ploughing, planting, reaping, sowing seed, and each season trying to improve their methods. As men came to live in cities they learned to stretch their lives from generation to generation, engaging in commerce, making roads, building houses, planting colonies, and raising temples fit for the worship of God their help in ages past and their hope for years to come. *[Progress from power to look ahead.]*

We are accustomed to think of Society as presented to us at its best, and civilized life is, it is true, that which is typical of man, but there are survivals of lower stages of development all over the globe and throw-backs everywhere in our midst. The street-seller from the slums renews his stock several times a day. Paper boys, flower girls, the thief, the prostitute, are living still on the level of pure savagery. The casual labourer is engaged by the day and often refuses to work more than three times a week, earning enough to keep himself going but saving nothing. The regular labourer and the artisan measure their work by the job, and jobs are arranged by their masters to make a chain of continuous employment. The merchant with his clerks calculates his business by the year, dividing it into wholesale and retail ; his travellers anticipate the seasons ; *[Class divisions—the type of work.]*

his capital tides him over slack times ; he clears off superfluous stock by periodical sales. The professional man
lives by the whole measure of his calling ; the doctor builds
up a practice ; the lawyer pushes his way slowly at the Bar ;
the journalist works up a connexion ; the author makes
a name. The student and the ruler, finally, labour for the
future by plans of work, by government, by policy, sometimes by the pure adventure of research, not knowing if the
journey through their strange seas of thought will lead any-
whither in this world. The type of work has a continually
lengthening span as it ascends in the scale, and social progress lies largely in eliminating the lower forms, by for-
bidding street selling, by decasualizing labour, by introducing machinery to set free handicraft, by banking to
store the results of industry for future use, by education to
train the power of thought to leap forward to the time to
come. The survival of so much savagery in our midst is
a serious drag-back to our social welfare.

The type of
worker.

For class differences with their contrasts in personal
dignity of life are directly dependent on the length of the
span of work done by men. A man's private life depends
largely on the conditions of his calling, as it forces him to
work more, or less, by forecast. This influence of occupation on character is emphasized by the periods at which
wages are paid, entailing corresponding scales of house-
keeping by the week, the quarter, or the year. It is
rendered wellnigh irresistible if education is broken off at
the stage of childhood at which life is lived naturally by
smaller units, when the child is reproducing the phases of
development through which humanity has passed before.[1]

---

[1] Cp. my *Principles of Parish Work* (Longmans), 1905, pp. 78 and 196–
202. The ideas in these pages were in part suggested by Walter Bagehot's
Economic Studies (Longmans), fifth impression, 1902. E. g. p. 225 : 'It
must be observed, too, that there is an intellectual element in the matter.
Besides the two kinds of wants, future and present, there is the faculty
of making the comparison. And the habits of some people's lives fit them
much more for this than those of others. An actor who is concerned

This is one of our chief criteria in social judgement. The type of man, and the value of what he does, is bound up with the length of his unit of work. How is it with the clergy, and with what they do ?

I

It is generally accepted as satisfactory if the clerical staff of a parish ' meets on Monday morning to arrange the work for the week ', though, by a Looking-Glass-Land kind of arrangement the announcements of what is to be done have been already made in church the day before, and cannot, of course, be changed. In some places methods still more akin to those of savage society are adopted, and curates will be told on Thursday that they are to preach the next Sunday, or the different parts of the service be apportioned in a hurried whisper as the choir is leaving the vestry.

Arranging the work by the week.

What would happen in a school where the masters changed their classes every week ? How much would the boys learn ? Or at a college in which the order of lectures was changed every seven days ? How would a business flourish that never anticipated the seasons, or a shop that never ordered its stock of straw hats till the warm weather came ? The accepted clerical method is about on a level with that of less intelligent artisans.

To arrange the work every week means that the work ' arranged ' consists merely of taking services and preaching sermons. The former could be just as well, and with a great saving of trouble and inconvenience, be arranged once for all. The effect on the latter is, at least, unfortunate.

The consequence on teaching.

with the momentary impression on passing audiences has nothing to bring the future close to him at all. An artisan has little more ; his daily work passes with the day. But a capitalist in business has the future ever brought home to him. He has to look into the future, perhaps a distant one, for the profits on the goods which he buys, and to find in the near future the money with which these goods are to be paid for. A banker, above all men, incessantly lives in the future. A man thus living in the future, has a greater disposition to provide for it.'

Individual sermons are necessarily made weak productions, since thought needs more than a week in which to mature. So sermons have become a byword for dullness. To ' sermonize ' is to prove yourself a bore. Jokes about sleeping during sermons are tiresome because they are so stale from repetition. Further, certain subjects never get treated in preaching because there is no special reason for deciding to deal with them on one Sunday more than another as, week by week, the opportunity comes round.[1] The people who come to church regularly remain in complete ignorance of many elementary tenets of the Church simply from lack of system and outlook, while the still greater ignorance of others can be gathered from the pages of popular novelists, or from the columns of the daily press.

In policy.   In policy, as well as in teaching, the harm can be seen. Abuses of long standing are not checked because to deal with them needs sustained effort and a definite plan. The unreality, or ' respectability ', of our services is complained of, but not remedied. The scandal of allowing just any one to stand as godparent shocks us from time to time ; and then we forget it. Each year we feel that a mere ten weeks ' preparation ' for Confirmation is unsatisfactory ; but it goes on. The approach to our altars is quite unguarded. Every now and then there is a flare up of indignation, as after the Kikuyu conference or the Bannister Thompson case,[2] but nothing is done. The Holy Week services dis-

[1] As, for instance, church finance, the meaning of marriage, and the impossibility of divorce *a vinculo*, what happened at the Reformation, the reasons why we believe in God, the ethics of betting, the evidence for the genuineness of the books of the New Testament, the duties of godparents, &c.

[2] This was the notorious case in which a man who had ' married ' his sister-in-law was refused the Sacrament and prosecuted the clergyman who withheld it.   One legal authority asked, with reference to this case, ' How could a person be called upon to repent of his sin if there had been no sin according to law ? '   Another asked, ' What was the result ' of the Act of 1907 legalizing such ' marriages ' ?   ' Surely to make that lawful

appoint us each year ; we feel that they are somehow wrong, but after Easter, they are forgotten till they are on us again. The seating of our churches generally makes kneeling almost impossible and destroys the beauty of their proportions ; we agree as to the fact, but that is all. Bad music reigns almost supreme ; trivial hymns are popular ; the people who are there resent new ones ; but the musical people who have been driven away would not know if we chose others next week, so the tradition of Dykes and Barnby remains unchallenged. On personal character the effect is no less sad. We used to be told that it was the continual starting that wore out the tram horses. Disjointed sermons, unconnected visiting from day to day, isolated efforts unrelated to any continuous purpose, prevent work from acquiring impetus as it goes. The work other than that of taking services or preaching, it is too often assumed, need not even be arranged by the week, so it resolves itself for the most part into promiscuous uncorrelated calling on people from house to house. Men get to rely on physical energy, as must all casual labourers. Like unskilled workmen they become ' too old at forty '. A deterioration of mental power and character too often follows. The difference becomes marked between them and men of other professions who were not so different from them when they were together at school or at college.[1]

On character.

matrimony which before was illicit cohabitation and incest with all its consequences.' Another declared that ' these marriages had been declared and were made (*sic*) contrary to God's law. The legislature now made them valid ' ; while yet another said that he was of opinion that a marriage ' which before was contrary to the laws of God, merely because the State condemned it as such, was so no longer, and that by virtue of the State which legalizes it ' ! By the side of such claims that attributed to the King of France in the order

' De par le Roy. Défense à Dieu
de faire miracle en ce lieu '

becomes comparatively moderate.

[1] *Principles of Parish Work*, p. 271.

II

There is not the least reason why this should be so. If only Church work were brought up to the level of that of the other higher departments of life, and each unit made longer in span, its character would at once be altered. To begin with the preaching of sermons : if, as in schools, at the end of the holiday season a plan were mapped out for the year, the teaching could be made at once more systematic and more varied. Men need to understand theology, Church customs, and Christian duty, and so a due proportion of doctrinal, devotional or ecclesiastical, and of moral sermons could be kept. The outlines of the Creed could be kept before the minds of the congregation, as indeed is now fairly well assured by the Church calendar ; Church customs could be explained once for all, instead of being sometimes dwelt upon with wearisome iteration and sometimes never touched on ; many practical and ethical questions which are at present ignored because, important as they are, it does not occur to the preacher to dwell on them on any one particular Sunday, would receive serious consideration at some time in the year.

This would enormously lighten the labour of preaching. The difficult thing—the ' parson's perplexity ' as the advertisement has it—is to choose a subject and to start. When once begun, sermons nearly always tend to be too long or too full of matter. But with a plan in his mind, the preacher could hold over what is superfluous for another sermon, and so one would lead on to the next. He would realize, as does the schoolmaster, how little can be got into one lesson, and how much is conveyed by steady connected work. As the singer has to learn to sing by phrases and not by isolated notes, as the grammarian learns that words have little beyond interjectory meanings unless in a sentence,[1]

---

[1] Augustine, *Confessions*, Bk. IV, ch. xi, § 17 ' Nam et quod loquimur per eundem sensum carnis audis; et non vis utique stare syllabas, sed transvolare, ut aliae veniant, et totum audias. Ita, semper omnia quibus

so the preacher would find each sermon grow in its content from its relation to the others. The interest would be greater because each would fall on prepared ground and have a greater 'apperception mass' ready to receive it. The value of the teaching would grow, since it would be more thorough, more varied, and would stimulate more thought.

It would soon be realized how much must be left out in the pulpit. We only find out how little we can get through, when we work with a syllabus. There is no time, for instance, on Sundays to teach the history as distinct from the message of the New Testament, still less that of the Old. It would at once become obvious that this must be done in the Day Schools, and that Sunday Schools are as inadequate for the purpose as a weekly sermon. We should get clear what should be taught there, and the master's lesson, which must be mainly historical, would at once gain an interest and religious meaning from its relation to worship and after-life. It would then be felt how little time or opportunity there is in the pulpit for more detailed work, and all sorts of subjects—Church History, apologetics, literary and critical study of the Bible, music, &c.—would be set aside for reading circles, lectures, or guild meetings, which would no longer be regarded, as is too often the case, both by clergy and people as mere occasions of boredom, since a real reason for their existence would have appeared. These in turn would soon need to be supplemented by reading and church magazine societies, and diocesan book clubs or libraries would be a natural outcome of this more systematized study.

Teaching outside the pulpit.

unum aliquid constat, et non simul sunt omnia ea quibus constat : plus delectant omnia quam singula, si possint sentiri omnia.' ('For even what I say unto thee, thou hearest by the same fleshly sense, yet dost thou not wish the syllables to stand still, no, but to fly away, that others may come and thou mayest hear the whole. It is the same with every unity that consists of a chain of parts. If it can be felt as a whole, the chain is more beautiful than the links.') Tr. C. Bigg in Methuen's *Library of Devotion*, p. 130.

The teacher, too, would grow mentally.   He would have
the strongest inducement to read, and the task of study
would become easier.   It may be the ideal that a man
should read for the sake of reading, and we all need at times
to do so with no utilitarian aim, but, as a matter of fact, the
chief reason in after life for pursuing a line of study is that
we want to teach, and the chief inducement to persevere
lies in the personal relationship of teacher and pupil.   Moreover, the quality of the work would improve when less
hurried and the outcome of slower moving thought.   The
preaching would become less a personal matter.   Its
interest would be shifted from the man to the message, and
congregations would not grow so tired of their clergy and of
their individual peculiarities.   But the first step necessary
to all this reform is to get rid of the attitude of mind which
is satisfied with ' meeting on Monday to arrange the work
of the week '.

III

The advantage of lengthening the unit of work is seen
most easily in the matter of sermons and teaching because
homiletics is the branch of Pastoral Theology that has been
most thought about and practised, but once the need of
plan is seen, and of time for things to work themselves
out, a similar change might be made in other parts of
our work.   Where, as things are now, we are beating
against the bars that cage us in and dissipating our energies,
we could by taking longer views save a vast amount of
friction and wasted energy.

We should learn to work with a purpose.   There is a general
feeling abroad that our Church services are not satisfactory.
We complain that they are too ' respectable ', though we
seldom go further and analyse what we mean by the word.
Clearly we do not want our Sunday morning congregations
to be disreputable, but having found a phrase we are
tempted to think that we have settled the difficulty.   Others
impressed with the apparent unreality of ' eleven o'clock

Mattins ' to the average congregation, or with the still more obvious spiritual breakdown of ' parade services ', have set themselves to a revival of the custom, universal till the Reformation, of Eucharistic worship, by substituting a ' High Celebration ' with ' non-communicating attendance ' as the chief Sunday service. This, with its unmistakeable insistence on worship as the prime reason for coming to church, has in many places evidently created the sense of reality that is sought for.

But such a change makes a big demand on their energies in carrying it out. There inevitably is opposition, and controversy and quarrels about such a matter are peculiarly painful to them as being concerned with what they hold most sacred. Many of their congregation leave. Others withdraw their support. It is best to make the change at once, they say ; so they face the consequences and carry their point only to find, after all, that they still have their whole work to do. They have alienated many of their best parishioners ; those who remain are for the most part only conforming. Tradition and associations are stronger than ideas and are slow to change. They find that many of those who still come to church do so merely because it is the ' eleven o'clock service ', and approve the change because there is more music and a greater number of hymns. They have not really grasped the principle of worship at the altar, as is shown by the fact that, if prevented from coming at eleven, it never occurs to them to come earlier. They only come at 7 a.m. or 8 a.m. if they intend to communicate.

The mistake has arisen from thinking by too short a unit of time. They have not realized how slowly men take in new ideas, and how still more slowly habits of spontaneous action establish themselves.

It would in most cases have been far better to have thought out a plan in advance, to have begun by encouraging attendance for worship at 7 or 8 a.m., the only time that the masses of working women and domestic servants can come to church on Sunday morning, and then gradually to have shifted the hour to 8.30 or 9, or even later, adding music and ceremonial as it comes (or does not come) naturally, watching to see what time suits people best, making arrangements for those who can only come at an earlier hour or prefer a simpler service, and so letting the religious side of human nature have its way and work out such customs as best express its devotion. This was the way that customs of public worship grew up in the past, and history is a safe guide to interpret human nature to-day. The strenuous method of sudden unthought-out change, besides being unsuccessful in itself, exhausts the reformer. ' Rows take too much out of you,' he says, ' I couldn't face such a task again,' and so other things equally crying out for attention are simply left not attempted.

Baptism and god-parents.

I have elsewhere suggested a method of gradually removing the present scandal connected with godparents and Baptism.[1] At one end of the social scale sponsors who ' stand for ' children obviously have not the slightest idea of what they are doing ; sometimes they are induced to be godparents by the promise of a drink before or after the ceremony. At the other end Roman Catholics who believe that the Church of England is a schismatical body, Quakers who are not christened themselves, Agnostics who believe neither in Sacrament nor God, are accepted as guarantors for children being made members of the Church, by Baptism, through faith in God. It was not altogether satisfactory that Huxley should have persuaded Sir Joseph Hooker to be godfather to his son by the promise that he could act if he preferred it by deputy saying, ' the clerk shall tell all the lies for you ' at ' the farce '. Still less so was it that any clergyman should have accepted him without apparently any inquiry into his good faith.[2]

[1] *Principles*, p. 133 ; *An Introduction to the Study of Pastoral Theology*, (Oxford), 1912, p. 74.

[2] *Life and Letters of T. H. Huxley*, vol. i, p. 223, Letter to Sir J. D. Hooker, January 3, 1861 : ' My wife and I have a great favour to ask of

Yet the proposed sudden remedies, such as that of refusing all but communicants as godparents, are simply impracticable. You cannot in a moment cure a long-standing abuse. The essential thing is to secure time both for a general reform, and for dealing with each particular case. The key to the situation lies in demanding proper notice of Baptism by a form of application. Then gradually pressure can be brought to bear and public opinion educated. · The standard of sponsorship can be slowly raised. First respectability can be insisted on, then religious sincerity and habits, and ultimately real churchmanship, and in the continuous visiting necessitated (not from house to house, but directed to a definite end) innumerable opportunities could be found of making suggestions or of explaining difficulties such as would work continuously towards a better understanding of the meaning of Baptism and of the nature of social Christianity. It would be a long process, but each visit would not stand isolated, as it would prepare for the next. The work might be tedious, but it would not be a mere frittering away of energy, and, no doubt, much of it could soon be delegated to others.

I have also suggested a similar remedy for our present inadequate method of ' preparation ' for Confirmation,[1] a rite for which practically no candidate is ever refused. The way to reform lies, I believe, in securing a much longer

Preparation for Confirmation.

you, which is neither more nor less than to stand godfather to our little son. You know my opinions of these matters, and I would not ask you to do anything I would not do myself, so if you consent, the clerk shall tell all the lies for you, and you shall be asked to do nothing else than to help devour the christening feed, and be as good a friend to the boy as you have been to his father. My wife will have the youngster christened, although I am always in a bad temper from the time it is talked about until the ceremony is over. The only way of turning the farce into a reality is by making it an extra bond with one's friends. On the other hand, if you have any objection to say " all this I steadfastly believe " even by deputy, I know you will have no hesitation in saying so, and in giving me as frank a refusal to my request.'

[1] *Principles*, pp. 137–47 ; *Pastoral Theology*, p. 74.

time of probation, a revival of the catechumenate for one, or, better still, for two years during which the candidate should be under supervision. The details in this scheme, as in that suggested above, might need to be modified or elaborated, but the point is that we need a clear, intelligible plan involving a longer outlook in the actual work, which, in turn, would make a sustained and effective policy possible. Nothing permanent is likely to be done by acting on the spur of the moment.

Fencing the altar.

As regards the approach to the altar our whole discipline is in abeyance. At most we have the precarious safeguard that most of our celebrations of the Holy Communion are early in the morning. But, as a matter of fact, Nonconformists who have no intention of seeking reception into the communion of the Church present themselves at the altar, and boast of it. Agnostics who retain a feeling for religious sentiment do the same. Persons who have defied the Christian law of marriage deliberately dare the clergy to repudiate them, and threaten actions for libel if they are so refused. It would be impossible suddenly to insist on notice in accordance with the rubric, yet at any moment a crisis may occur over this very question.

A plan must be made and steadily tried. We must feel our way, do nothing in a hurry, but delay in nothing : for reforms take time. Probably the first step is to make an Easter Communion list asking for notice from those intending to communicate. This is already done in many parishes. Then the practice might be extended to Whit-Sunday and Christmas. Then a general permission might be given to all who are members of parish guilds. They would be the more frequent communicants and would be well known, so that in their case to give notice on each several occasion would be unnecessary. Then, possibly (and especially if the number of worshippers who are present without then communicating were found to grow) some arrangement might be made for intimating an intention to communicate either at the offertory[1] while the collection is being made, or at the door of the church. References from fellow churchmen, or commendations from the clergy of other parishes, might be demanded of new-comers, or of those who attach themselves to churches other than that of the parishes in which they live. This would necessitate clear notices of explanation, such as all strangers would not fail to see, an open church where forms of inti-mation of intention to communicate could be filled up, and a great deal of visiting on the part of the clergy, but, again, all this labour would be directed to a definite end.

No one can travel through the country without noticing how many of our finest churches are spoiled by their incon-gruous seating, or without realizing how unlikely it is that any one will use for private prayer a place of worship that is filled with heavy rows of seats stretching over its whole area. *Seating.*

For when the old pews were got rid of the reform was in most cases not carried far enough. Our seats rarely allow enough room for a full-sized man. They are dirty, since they are seldom open underneath. They are entirely unsuited for children. They dwarf our churches, bringing down the roof by their horizontal lines, and burying the bases of the pillars, and they destroy all sense of space by covering the whole area from east to west right up to the very doors. Moreover they are primarily *seats*, and as such offer a direct discouragement to kneeling, for they are the outcome of a false theory of church-going, namely that we go to ' get good ' rather than to worship. They are suited only for one time and place, namely the eleven o'clock service on Sunday morning. For children's services, for funerals, for weddings, for confirmations, for the daily offices, even for celebrations of the Holy Communion, when communicants must leave their places to go up to the altar,

[1] At present the collectors of the alms generally roughly estimate the number by counting those who contribute.

they are quite unsuited. They encourage passivity by their continuous invitation to sit still and look on. They rigidly check all freedom of motion or variety in bearing or posture.

Our reforms in this matter have seldom got beyond the substitution of chairs, and these are disliked by some. Even chairs when they are joined together have many of the disadvantages of fixed seats; yet loose chairs are even more strongly objected to by many. But, surely, there is no reason why the one or the other alternative should be exclusively adopted, and rigid uniformity spread over the whole church. People are of different sizes and of varied temperaments. The obvious thing is to have benches for those who like benches, fixed chairs for those who like fixed chairs, loose chairs or *prie-Dieu* for those who like to be free, even open spaces for those who like to stand.

Such variety, almost universal abroad and at once recognized by travellers as the right thing, is difficult to secure in England. Tradition blocks the way. The seats are there, and men have very little imagination. Moreover it does not do to force your ideas on people. The best plan, therefore, is to create the proper conditions in which a better state of things can grow. What is impossible in a church as a whole is easy in a side-chapel. As in our cathedrals, where the naves are deserted and bare and the choirs corded up, the lady chapel is often obviously a place of worship put to the uses for which it was built, so a well arranged side-chapel would set an ideal before the eyes of the general congregation, and gradually its influence could be extended till the whole was modelled on its pattern. If, as seems to be the case, an immense spiritual issue is involved we should begin at once, as the growth will take time.[1]

Holy Week services.
Year by year, as Holy Week comes round, many churchmen feel that there is something wrong. The regular choir

[1] For a fuller working out of this subject see *The Commonwealth* for November 1916.

offices are set aside. Just at the season at which we should expect the Church to sing her most solemn and appealing music, the services become dreary without being pathetic. The daily offices are hurried through in the afternoon, and their place in the evening, when the masses can come, is taken by metrical litanies with multiplied addresses, or by the *Story of the Cross*, or perhaps Stainer's *Crucifixion* is sung. The collapse of liturgical worship shows how far it is from having become really natural to us. The Three Hours' Service on Good Friday only suits some ; to others it is a terrible infliction—and no alternative for the time from twelve to three is offered. The general public goes to concerts and likes to listen to the *Messiah*. The need for something more is felt, but the efforts to meet it are not successful. To borrow the Roman Office of Tenebrae, part of an all-year system of many daily offices, is to take a thing meaningless to us. Even the great processions that have been organized in London and elsewhere are in imminent danger of being spoiled by our besetting desire to edify others, in being spoken of as ' a great means of impressing the indifferent crowds '. Each year there are a few complaints in the Church papers, but nothing is done. No notes of what was felt to be wanted are taken at the time to serve for guidance in the following year. After Easter the whole question is put aside. But, surely, Holy Week should be the time when our familiar liturgical offices should receive their most solemn rendering with their largest congregations. Even in the Roman Church, where the Latin Breviary Offices have ceased to be followed by the people except on Sunday afternoon, the Mattins Offices of Holy Week have held their place, and have gathered round them some of the finest Church music and of the most popular, if not otherwise noteworthy, ceremonial. Surely what we want is some elaboration of the usual service, say, by the singing of antiphons to each psalm for the day, some setting of the lessons to music with soli and Chorus as was done by

Bach in his Passion Music, some interweaving of the different parts with lyrical refrains in the shape of hymns sung by the people. In addition, human nature, if we may judge by customs of other lands and ages, seems to demand something in the way of procession and pilgrimage, a going to deck the graves in churchyards, a journey to some symbolic shrine in the country or from one church to another in the town, or some services in church which will serve as a definite profession of Christianity by those who take part in them, something to mark time, to keep men occupied and together, feeling their common union in Christ, something that can be sustained where continuous prayer or preaching is too great a strain. What exactly would interpret English devotion must perhaps be found out by experiment. It is not likely to be the same as the customs of foreign lands. But before the right opportunities and conditions can be secured for such to grow there must be much drawing up of proposed forms, much selecting of antiphons, much composing and practising of music—a matter of repeated experiment and observation year by year, demanding continued study of liturgical principles on the part of the clergy, a careful training of students in liturgiology, so that they may know what prayers and forms to select from the immense treasury of devotion stored up in ancient sacramentaries or in living foreign rites of East and West, and, above all, that they may catch the right spirit and instinct of liturgical fitness.

Church music.

Severe strictures are passed upon our art in church by people who know. We talk of the conflict of religion and science, but doctors are often churchwardens while artists are, as a rule, hopelessly alienated from religion. It is not satisfactory that a lecturer on poetry, himself one of our foremost English poets, should assume that because a hymn is poetry it will not be found in any of our modern hymnals,[1]

[1] So Sir Henry Newbolt, in a lecture on ' Poetry and Politics ' delivered before the English Association on June 21, 1912. As a matter of fact the

that a popular novelist should write about ' a pretty little tune, such as they sang in church ',[1] or that a conductor of a famous choral society should rebuke his choir for bad singing by asking ' How many of you sing in Church choirs ? ' [2]

But in contemplating a reform we are met with the fact that our present congregations are in possession and they are at least to be considered. It is easy to alienate them, but to do so will not of itself bring in the others. They are familiar with certain hymns. They know, and are fond of, certain tunes. These may be bad, but they have gathered to themselves certain associations which the stronger words and more dignified harmonies have not got.

Therefore the work of reform must be the work of a generation. We must begin with the children and let them form new associations round good and worthy music set to fine and noble words. Similar work is being done in the Schools. Children are proving capable of appreciating Shakespeare to their immense gain in after life. We must give them the best, not as is at present generally the case, the most trivial and vulgar. We must get rid of the majority of special Children's Hymn Books with their doggrel verse and catchy tunes. Future value must outweigh present convenience. We must get the best players

hymn in question, ' Jerusalem, my happy home,' in its original form is to be found in *The English Hymnal*, No. 638, though not, as he rightly complained, in the majority of collections. Sir Charles Villiers Stanford in his *Pages from an Unwritten Diary*, writes : ' The worst sign of the times is the modern hymn-tune. It represents for the Church the equivalent of the royalty ballad for the concert room.' Mr. Robert Bridges in a paper ' About Hymns ', written for the Church Music Society (Occasional Paper, No. 11), urges that the clergy ' should have at least one service a week where people like myself can attend without being offended or moved to laughter '.

[1] E. F. Benson, *Arundel*, p. 117.

[2] It is only fair to state that the conductor of the choir in question was in no small degree prompted to his question by his high standard as to what is required in the service of religion.

that we can for our children's services, and not use them as good opportunities for beginners to get used to the organ. We must get those who do it well to play and sing solos to our boys and girls in the schools, or we must bring them to church to hear them, and so familiarize them from the first with all the best music, so that in after life the songs and choruses of the *Messiah*, or even of Bach's Passion music, the cadences of plain-song hymns and ancient chorales, shall be as familiar to them as are our national English, Scottish, Irish, and Welsh airs, or the great speeches of Shakespeare. There is much to be done, so we should begin at once, steadily weeding out bad tunes and hymns and steadily substituting good ones in their place.[1]

The use of the open church.

The above are a few ways in which greater continuity in ordinary parish work is demanded and would be fruitful of great results. Many others might be instanced. The use of the open church is not entirely dependent on seating arrangements, even if our present methods form an initial bar. In many other ways we are far from the ideal. We open churches ' in the dinner hour ' or from 11 a.m. to 4 p.m., just the times, as we might know from our own experience if we would but question it, when no one is likely to want to go in. We leave the main door locked, or only open one of its two divisions, oblivious of the fact that this is a recognized warning in banks and shops that people

---

[1] *Life and Letters of Edward Thring*, G. R. Parkin (Macmillan), 2nd ed., p. 305 : ' I am so glad you do something special for the children. What a frightful mistake the Church Services have generally been for them, and the way they have been treated in church.

' I often think of the Bristol cutler, Plum. My brother was in his shop talking to him, and a boy came in to buy a knife. Plum left my brother (who was rather a swell) and paid extraordinary attention to suiting the boy with a knife to his mind. When he had finished, my brother remarked on the pains he had taken. " Why, you see, sir," he said, " that knife's a great matter to a boy ; if I give him a good one he'll remember it as long as he lives, and always come to me again." A fine and true philosophy—always give children a good one. Alas ! how often, how universally, forgotten.'

are not to enter as closing time is near. We need to begin
with the children and systematically set ourselves to make
the use of the church natural to the next generation, sending
them in on special occasions such as Rogation Days, days of
intercession for foreign missions, on birthdays or after sickness, when we find they have omitted to say their prayers
that morning (for in after life they will often find it harder
still to do so at home), giving them opportunities of offering
flowers in church or of making a record of visits by filling
up with crosses a paper hung up and ruled in squares for the
purpose—childish practices, perhaps, but as such suitable
for children.

The first step in these and in many other reforms is the
lengthening of the span of work by doing things on the scale
of the month or of the year, with plans stretching out over
several years, instead of by the week or even by the day.
Subsidiary to this the study of history will be found of
value. For history reveals the gradual growth of institutions and shows how slow they were to establish themselves.
To read the story of the past is an excellent antidote for
impatience and discouragement. Many a practical suggestion can be gained from study of liturgical and pastoral
Theology in the records of other days. The slow growth
of the Calendar, some days being observed universally and
from the beginning and others only finding a partial acceptance after the passing of centuries, will guide us in estimat-
ing how far we can expect, or wish, various saints' days to
be observed to-day. The tendency of ecclesiastics to
multiply them, easily traceable in the history of the Breviary in the Middle Ages, reappears to-day and needs, just as
it needed then, to be checked. The story of the slow growth
of the use of private confession and the regulation of its
use, suggests much in the presence of the continually
pressing of it by certain of the clergy to-day, and its close
original connexion with Church discipline raises the question
whether the present purpose of its advocates is not mainly

Value of the study of history.

evangelical, namely the desire to help the penitent by influence and advice, and as such an entirely different thing (though not therefore necessarily a bad one) from the more Catholic custom. If daily services originally arose chiefly out of customs of private prayer which gradually became prayer in common and public, the fact is full of significance when we are trying to revive and extend the custom in our own day.[1]

Need of keeping records.

If the study of the past is valuable the study of history in the making is even more imperative. For continuity with the immediate past is almost a necessary condition of continuity in work in the immediate future. This has been found to be the case in all effective social work. Poor Law officials, Care Committee workers, and Hospital Almoners, have to keep case papers and diaries; otherwise, without a continuous record of what has already been done, there can be no sustained action. This is but one example of how what has been found necessary in business life is also found necessary in social work. An obvious corollary of all that has been said above is that there must be in our parishes some careful system of keeping of parish records, of some form of diaries and case papers, not only for workers to refer to themselves about the details of their past work but to ensure some chance of this continuity that is so much needed through inevitable changes in the staff, or in ordinary chances of the varying conditions of our daily life.[2]

[1] Cp. my *Matins and Evensong* (The Faith Press), 1920, ch. i.
[2] *Principles of Parish Work*, ch. iii.

CHAPTER II

THE AREA OF WORK

' No man who is not inflamed by vainglory into enthusiasm, can flatter himself that his single, unsupported, desultory, unsystematic endeavours are of power to defeat the subtle designs and united cabals of ambitious citizens. When bad men combine, the good must associate ; else they will fall one by one, an unpitied sacrifice in a contemptible struggle.'— EDMUND BURKE, *Thoughts on the Cause of the Present Discontents*, Works (*World's Classics*, 1906, vol. ii, pp. 78–9).

THE advance of the world has not come from the power to look ahead alone ; power of combination has also been an important factor in progress. Large undertakings require more than persistence ; they need width of outlook. This has been specially impressed upon us by the change brought about by the industrial revolution. *Progress from wider outlook.*

The invention of machinery, especially when applied to utilize the newly discovered power of steam and, in more recent years, of electricity, has resulted in an enormous saving of labour and, at the same time, in an immense increase of wealth. Industrial undertakings are now planned on a much larger scale than of old and employ a far greater number of men. This has necessitated their living together in greater numbers and has so caused the growth of large towns. Where in the days of home industries and of small farms men were gathered in cities mainly for the work of distribution alone, now production is also seated in the centres of population. The country has, it is true, been developed, but the most prominent feature in the change has been the moving of the centre of gravity to the towns. *Change from the industrial revolution.* *In the scale of work.*

The nature of the work has been altered as well as its scale. Intelligence now counts for more than mere industry. There is greater elaboration in the means of produc- *In the character of work.*

tion, and more differentiation between the various parts of the work. Agriculture is spread over large areas by the development of means of distribution. Railways have made possible the farms of Canada, where the farmer besides growing corn has to know about markets in far distant centres. Greater co-operation between workers is required, both of producers in the factory itself and of distributors outside—of travellers, of buyers, and of retail salesmen. The connexion of one part of the work with another must be realized by the manager. One factory learns from another. Experts meet together to consult for the interests of the whole trade. Imagination, breadth of view, and the power of carrying several things at once in the mind, are factors which count in the present day.

Complexity of society.

Answering to this growing complexity of manufacture is a growing complexity of society itself. There are far more sources of influence in the life of each family. Each member probably works all day in a different shop where, for so many hours, different thoughts are in the air and different standards of life accepted. These brought home at night form an intellectual and moral combination that cannot be understood unless a sufficiently wide outlook is secured. For evil or good the ordinary events of life are conditioned by a combination of influences operating in widely separated areas. Further, the greater strenuousness of organized work impels workers to seek more, and more varied, recreation, thus bringing in yet fresh strands of interest and new experiences into the whole. The area of life and work has been enormously widened for society as a whole.

That is to say the world, for the great mass of men, has become larger. There is everywhere more necessity for co-operation and organization. More enters into the purview of each family, and life itself has grown more complex. In this general change how do we stand in church matters?

I

Of necessity our chief work has moved from the country to the town, and with its larger parishes, its larger populations, the work is on a larger scale. But, for the most part, there has been merely an enlargement and not a development of country methods. As this has been made with little thought about their original fitness to their circumstances, the result has been unfortunate. The natural feudal relationships of the country have disappeared, but the external symptoms of them have been continued and multiplied arithmetically. The friendly visit of persons already closely connected by local ties has become a system of house-to-house visitation. The spontaneous gift of the employer's wife to the wife of the employed has become a matter of doles bestowed by ' kind ladies ' for which, it is believed, you must qualify by going to church or to a mothers' meeting. The hospitality of the teacher to his class has become a ' day in the country '. Only a fraction of the people are touched by these methods since the industrial change has affected men and the workshop more than the family and the school, and ' church work ' has become a matter that deals almost entirely with women.

In the parish.

Country methods merely enlarged.

There is no delegation of work such as that on which the life of the factory depends. The vicar still retains the method of cottage industries, utilizing the services of his wife and perhaps a handy man. He tries to do everything himself, and is worn out by excessive occupation with detail. The only imagery by which his work is described as pastoral is drawn from industrial conditions of ancient Palestine, though, to-day, sheep-farming in Australia is an entirely different thing. The consequence is that few fellow-workers are used, and the best find no scope in the work they are asked to do. As they say, they are capable of something better than ' knocking at people's doors and telling them it is a fine day '.

No delegation of work.

Overlapping.

For the effective work of an office it is recognized that each must have his work and his responsibility. In a large household each servant has his or her definite task. But in the parish the different members of the staff overlap one another in their work ; each works very largely in ignorance of what the others are doing. Sunday Schools and Day Schools go on side by side without any co-operation. Each member of a family is approached by a different worker and some by several. The District Visitors, the C.E.M.S., the boys' club and the girls' club, the Sunday School, the choir, the Guilds, the Mothers' meeting, all send their representatives knocking at the same door. The loss of power is enormous if they are all pulling different ways. Visitors in different districts give relief on different scales. If the School Care Committee adopts one policy the lady at the mothers' meeting goes behind it and upsets their plans. It is bad enough within the parish but worse outside, where rival choirs compete for boys with good voices, and the member of the club suspended for bad behaviour finds ready admission in another a few streets away. Like Tityrus we have simply thought of London as a large village,[1] and the church work of to-day is ludicrously simple in the face of the complexity of society.

II

Need of correlation.

What is needed is a proper correlation of the different parish activities and of the forces that they are based upon. We want a wider outlook and a larger unit in the area of work.

Within the Church.

This correlation must begin in the church itself, first between the members of the staff and then between the various parts of the congregation.

Members of the staff.

There should be a settled method of taking the services.

[1] Cp. Vergil, *Bucolica*, Ecl. i. 19 :

Urbem, quam dicunt Romam, Meliboee, putavi
stultus ego huic nostrae similem.

If it is argued that if one man always officiates at the same time there is a danger that people will consider, and ' run after ', the man, the answer surely is that this must be remedied by impersonality in leading common prayer. The officiant must sink himself in his office and forget himself and congregation in the presence of God. Individual eccentricities are out of place at the altar, but they are not corrected, or their harm removed, by spreading them over each Office in turn.

There should be co-ordination in the teaching in sermons. If the preachers are constantly being changed about it reduces their message to the lowest common measure of all. It is no justification for such a practice to say ' all are preaching the same thing ', since each ought to have something of his own to say. For each to repeat what the other says would be most tedious ; rather each should contribute his quota to a whole. This is what is done by the teaching staff of a school, where the different subjects are apportioned to various teachers with special qualifications but make together a complete curriculum. It is done by the staff of a College where the different points of view of each lecturer help to a realization of a study as a whole. The problem of securing unity in diversity, if a difficult, is a familiar one, and should not merely be shirked in the pulpit or at the altar.

A similar co-ordination is required in the parts of the services themselves. Frequently the Revised Version is quoted in the pulpit while the old ' Authorized ' is read from the lectern, and there is much tiresome waste of time caused by explaining the difference between the two. It does not much matter whether the *Gloria Patri* is said each verse alternately by priest and people, or if both verses are said by them together, nor whether it is said facing the East, or without change of posture ; but there should clearly be one position, and the same method, when the service is said and when it is sung. There should be no such striking

On public worship.

difference between the speaking and the singing voice such as is commonly heard. These are small points, perhaps, but they contribute to a mental incoherence which is all the more pervading because it is not consciously felt and resisted.

Choir and congrega-tion.

Similarly, there should be no dislocation of action between the choir and the congregation. Both should sit and stand together unless their parts in the service are related by deliberate contrast, as, for example, in an anthem ending with a chorale to join in which the congregation stands up. A pitch and pace should be assured that allows both to take part in the singing, unless by alternation two different kinds of music are brought into harmony. The music should never be allowed to interrupt the course of the service as is the case, for example, when the priest is kept waiting at the altar while the choir sings a too long setting of the *Benedictus qui venit* after the *Sanctus*. Children, if they have a special service, should use the same hymn-book and the same tunes as their elders, should learn the same responses, should become accustomed to the same general forms of worship, and should be familiarized with the same places of prayer that will be theirs in after life. Otherwise a dislocation is inevitable in their spiritual growth. Such divergence of interests and contradictions of idea would be noticed far more readily if the clergy more often sat in the body of the church, or if choristers and organists from time to time took their places with the congregation they would more readily see things from the peoples' point of view.

Co-ordina-tion outside the church.

From co-ordination of detail within the church we may pass on to correlation of the church with things outside. To begin with the school and with details : The method of saying the Lord's Prayer should be the same in the two. If

In the school.

children are accustomed to one pace, to one method of punctuation, or one way of intoning, in school, it causes a certain distraction if different methods are adopted in church. The hitch can quite easily be removed. If different methods of voice production are adopted and the same children are taught in school to sing softly with the natural ' chest ' voice with which they speak, and are trained in the choir to use only the artificial ' head ' voice because of its greater resounding properties, especially on the vowel ' oo ', the result will not be the best either from the artistic or the religious point of view. Probably in many cases both church and school would profit if the schoolmaster took in hand the whole singing in church, and led it with the whole body of boys and girls rather than the ' choir '. If when children are brought to church from the school they enter by a door that is locked at other times, it will not accustom them to enter the church in the usual way either privately or for Sunday worship. If they are marched in two and two for the sake of order, it must be remembered that it will help them much sometimes to be allowed to come in by themselves as they will have to do when they grow up.

In broader issues and in bigger matters church and school should be brought together. The interpretation of the Old Testament as subsidiary to the New is generally that found in church, while many schools are giving a quite dispro-portionate attention to the Old, and teaching it on anti-quated methods based on a traditional theory of verbal inspiration which the teachers themselves no longer believe. ' Prayer Book lessons ' are likely to be dull and meaningless unless they are connected with coming to church. ' Learn-ing to find places in the Prayer Book ' is a useless exercise unless something is to be done with them when they are found. Church study on the lines of nature study is profit-able for children who are interested in things they see but bored by talk about abstract ideas which they cannot yet understand.[1] If the last year's work in school were directed

---

[1] See an admirable series of lessons by Miss M. E. Penstone, published by the National Society under the title *Church Study*.

definitely to preparation for Confirmation on its religious side it would give it point and do much to bridge over the gap between school conditions and independent religious life.[1]

Church, school, and Sunday school. Similarly, church, school, and Sunday school should work together. The lessons on Sunday, or the address at the children's service, would gain in meaning if they were based on the week-day lessons, and the church might take the place for the masses that Rugby chapel took for Dr. Arnold's boys.[2] The hymn practice on Friday morning might well be of the actual hymns and parts of the service to be sung on the following Sunday. The school methods of teaching and discipline and the words of order (or the absence of them) should be the same in school and in church, for the children in each are the same.[3]

School and mothers' meeting. Similarly the school and the mothers' meeting (or the school for mothers, or whatever is to take the place of that rather antiquated institution if it proves incapable of reform)[4] should help one another. The interest of the parents is the best force for securing regular attendance. The meaning and purpose of education, about which the mass of Englishmen have so few clear ideas, questions of health, of future work, of home prayers, of moral training,

[1] Cp. J. J. Findlay, *Principles of Class Teaching* (Macmillan), 1911, ch. ix, ' The Last Years of the Primary School,' where the similar problem in general education is considered, namely, that of (p. 218) ' the gulf between the pursuits of home and the pursuits of school which must somehow be bridged over '.

[2] Cp. A. P. Stanley, *Life and Letters of Doctor Arnold of Rugby* (Ward, Lock & Co.'s Minerva Library, pp. 88–95). Cp. also Matthew Arnold's ' Rugby Chapel '.

[3] For a warning against unintelligent copying of the externals of week-day school discipline see *The Teacher's Craft in Church and School*, by M. E. Penstone, Hetty Lee, and R. Holland. National Society, 1912, pp. 2–12.

[4] Cp. below, p. 154, ' As others see us—Mothers' Meetings.' For suggestions of ways in which the mothers' meeting might be made a really useful institution, see *New Methods in the Mothers' Meeting*, by Mrs. E. Paget (Longmans), 1915.

of child psychology (called by the simpler name of child study) could be well treated there in connexion with the actual work of the teachers and the Care Committee. Arrangements could be made for the parents to visit the schools, which they would now see with very different eyes from those with which they saw them as children. If the parents could be got to come to the week-day childrens' services, when they bring their little ones to the school door, or to take them into the church on the way for a few words of private prayer, the spiritual gain to them, to their children, and to the nation at large would be enormous. It is simply a question of combination of forces.

Similarly school, church, and clubs should be brought together. At present their connexion is not thought out, though Scouts' corps and Boys' Brigades are generally working in close connexion with the school, with results of success conspicuous in contrast with the older methods of ' boys' clubs ' to ' get hold of rough lads '. The two rival theories of such institutions, that of keeping together the best so as to make a strong centre of Christian influence and life, and that of trying to bring influence to bear on the worst, have seldom been thought out, though entirely different methods are necessary for the one and for the other. The relations of each, too, to the rest of the organic life of the Church, are no less different, the one centring round guilds and the Sacrament, the other round Sunday afternoon classes and sermons.

Church, school, and club.

In another direction the co-ordination of two activities, which at present go their own ways, would surely be most effective. If in the parish magazine syllabuses of the sermons to be preached could be published beforehand, as is done by University Extension Lecturers, interest would be awakened. This, of course, depends on the adoption of the longer span of work that we considered in the last chapter. Lists of books might also be published in the next number after the sermons had been preached for

The parish magazine.

those who were anxious to think more about the matters dealt with. One of the most successful features of the Pan-Anglican Conference of 1908, and one which contributed in no small degree to its usefulness, was the issue of pamphlets by far-seeing Committees in good time before the actual meetings.

Language and pronunciation.

The language, and the ideas that go with the language, used in church, must not be disjoined from that used outside. It is unfortunate to have one pronunciation for singing and another for speaking, for it brings a sense of unreality into one or the other. Still more is it unfortunate to have a church pronunciation different from that of secular life. To say or sing ' See-own ' for Sion, is to cut off our worship from all the rich associations that have gathered in literature round the name of the Holy City, and have become part and parcel of our English heritage of thought. To sing ' marn ' for man, or ' tee-r ' and ' fee-r ' for tear and fear, or to express a wish for a touch of a ' varnished hand ' instead of a vanished one, because such sounds are supposed to be easier to sing, is to fence off music as having nothing to do with ordinary rational intelligent life. It is not perhaps a serious matter if opera seems silly even if the artistic loss is great. In religion it *is* serious.

Co-ordination with secular institutions.

So, again, with secular institutions in the parish or district. The Church, if we had a wider view, would learn to co-operate with them. At present we are often hindering the work of evening classes by our rival clubs, but if Church organizations for boys and girls really whole-heartedly set to work, how much they might do for education, and if men and women from the church were really interested in continuation schools how much they might do to help their social and human side. Public libraries are made centres of propaganda by cranks of all sorts ; the Church should at least see that her newspapers are in the reading rooms for those who wish to consult them, that such standard works are on their shelves as the clergy may wish to refer to in

their sermons, or to direct inquirers to who may wish to
satisfy themselves on different points of Christian evidence
or doctrine.   School and parish banks are of little use by
themselves;   connected with the work of Friendly Societies
they might do a real and lasting service to the cause of
working-class thrift and life, and as helping the nation in
time of stress they were found far more effective than any
poster or appeal to subscribe to war loans.   The Press is
hardly made use of, though doubtless the local paper would
always be glad of copy of the right sort and would distribute
automatically news and ideas that we fail to make reach the
ears and eyes of the public.

The leaders in the whole network of social activities are
only too anxious to make use of the services of Church
workers of the right sort, and are ready to do so as soon as
they have made some study of economic principles and have
had some definite training in social work.   Any such bridg-
ing over the chasm that lies between the Church and the
outside world would open up channels of communication
for religious force to make itself felt throughout Society.
We should not ' get hold of ' these institutions, or wish to
do so, but we might well permeate them with the Christian
spirit.

III

When the different forces within the parish have been
brought into relation to one another we shall be in a position
to bring them to bear on abuses and defects outside in
a combined attack.

Combined attack on abuses.

Thus, a certain proportion of our communicants make
a point of being in church some ten minutes before, and of
staying some ten minutes after the service, to make their
preparation and thanksgiving.   But they are the minority
and, it would almost appear, a decreasing minority.   The
greater number come in at the last moment and go out in
a body the instant the priest leaves the altar.   You can

In devotion.

even in many places see young lads hanging about outside chattering instead of coming in. This is a bad preparation for the act of communion, and the loss where there is no general habit of remaining in church for a time after is incalculable, as here is probably just the centre from which spontaneous devotion can spread and grow.

It is true that vague recommendations are from time to time made from the pulpit suggesting better things, but they too often come near to mere nagging. Instead of such, a combined effort should be made when it seems the right time to take the question in hand. A sermon should be preached entirely dealing with the question, pointing out the seemliness of preparation and thanksgiving, with illustrations from liturgiology, history, or biography, and the ten minute rule should be definitely recommended. This should be backed up by the provision of manuals and leaflets at a shelf or table near the door, by some notes written clearly and pointedly in the Parish Magazine, by special emphasis at each of the guilds in turn, and the occasion chosen should, perhaps, be that when similar advice is being given to the recently confirmed who, in pre- paring for their First Communion, would be so much helped (it might be pointed out) by the example of their elders. For evils can be attacked by example as well as precept, and the attacker should be specially careful to see that he makes his own preparation and thanksgiving before and after celebrating, and that he observes silence in the vestry till the latter has been made. His churchwardens, servers, and choir will soon get to understand why he does not talk to them, and will probably learn to follow his example. If the bad custom of leaving the church as soon as the cele- brant has gone from the altar has established itself, much can be done to destroy it by seeing to it that the verger does not rattle keys or open doors, as if ordering people out so that he may get home to his breakfast, and by getting a certain few individuals deliberately to wait on their knees to counteract the contagious impulse of the mass of the congregation to rise and go out.

The unreality of much of our worship is widely felt, but the feeling only, as a rule, discharges itself in epigrams about ' glorified matins ', ' anglicanism ', and ' respectability ', or in irritable complaints and sermons about ' indifference '. Instead of such peevish talk the evil complained of should be analysed. Its causes will be found to be various, some physical, some psychological, and some moral. Among the physical causes is probably to be reckoned the general, unconscious, irreverence of attitude brought about by the matter alluded to in the last chapter, namely, the spiritually depressing appearance of our churches, due to their seating arrangements. Among the psychological causes will be found the over-unfamiliarity with the forms of worship which has made attention difficult because there is so little variety in them. Among the more serious moral causes must be reckoned the fact that we have far too often allowed ourselves to use words without meaning what we say.

Unreality of worship.

The attack must be made, then, in concert from all sides, material, intellectual, and spiritual. We must get, as we saw in the last chapter, more space and more sense of space, more variety in accommodation and more freedom. We must cut off bars from underneath chairs if we find they prevent kneeling. We must provide, or ask the congregation to provide, a sufficiency of hassocks. If the look of the church is depressing and ' undevotional ' we can probably at once widen our chancels, and give them greater dignity, by setting the choir stalls further back. We must make our schemes for beautifying the church (of course under the guidance of an expert architect with good taste), asking for gifts from the people and letting them know what is wanted. We must encourage men to use the open church—for nothing so furnishes a bare church as the sight of people kneeling in it—training our children to do so before self-consciousness makes it difficult.

Interest can be reawakened in part through sermons. We can ask our congregation ' What was to-day's lesson about ? Why was it chosen ? What do the words of the Te Deum mean ? ' We can urge them to stand up and to kneel properly together and with the choir as forming one body, for in the Army we have learned the connexion of drill and alertness. We can begin to read the Revised Version (if we do not do so already) not merely for its greater accuracy and beauty, but also to startle people by its unfamiliar phrases, and make them notice the meaning of what is read.[1] We can change the music, introducing plain-song, and so making the words of the Psalms, hitherto deprived of all meaning by the false accent of Anglican chants as commonly sung, start out into new significance. We can introduce a hymn-book whose higher literary standard will force a comparison with the weak verse that we have been contented to pay no attention to. If the book cannot be changed, we can exercise rigid care in the selection of hymns, and see at least that nothing is put into the mouths of men to sing that they cannot possibly mean. We can abolish the custom 'of singing ' Amen ' indiscriminately, whether the last verse is a doxology or not and regardless of whether it has any meaning in connexion with the words that have just gone before.[2] We can abolish the mechani-

---

[1] ' Englishmen should be sincerely modest about their own advantages, but it is worth while to remember that there is nothing in any other language to be compared with the Revised Version. We are sceptical about those famous cadences (of the Authorized Version). Their magnificence is undoubted, but was there no monotony in them ? ' A. Nairne, ' Versions of Holy Scripture ', *Church Quarterly Review*, July 1914, p. 439. Cp. M. de Saci quoted in Sainte-Beuve's *Port-Royal*, Hachette, 1860, Bk. II, ch. xvii, vol. ii, p. 325, ' On oublie que la véritable éloquence est dans les choses, et non dans les expressions,' and Diderot, quoted in J. Morley's *Recollections*, vol. i, p. 94 : ' Without technique, no painting, to be sure ; but when all is said I like ideas and the rendering and interpretation of them better than colour.'

[2] I have heard a choir sing :

Just and holy is thy name,
I am all unrighteousness ;

cal irreverence of the vestry prayer, and instead can keep the choir from talking for a few minutes by explaining to them the rationale of the day's office, why the lessons were chosen, or how the introits prepare for and the graduals and hymns carry on the lesson of the gospel. We can provide Bibles for the men of the choir so that during the lessons they can have something else to look at than the music they are just going to sing, or the advertisements of its covers. With each change the reason should be made clear, with the general aim of bringing back reality into the service in all its different parts. *Expliquez toujours* should be the motto of the church reformer.

Serious harm to the cause of religion is done by bad administration of charity ; harm in the results of over-lapping, of pauperizing, of encouragement of cant, of alienating the best and most self-respecting, of creating a general attitude of passivity and dependence. The symptoms of the evil are widespread and the causes many. In addition to sustained effort to counteract the evil, a combination of counter-forces is needed. We may begin almost anywhere. We may, for instance, start with refusing to sign papers and dispensary letters that are brought to us by persons about whom we know nothing. It will be necessary continually to explain that we cannot sign statements which are not true, or recommend persons as in need without inquiring into their affairs. But a mere negative policy is not enough. In the case of application for medical relief we can back up our action by calling attention to provident dispensaries and Friendly Societies.[1] At the same time we can forward schemes for training parish workers in elementary social science. We can insist on some knowledge

Bad administration of charity.

> False and full of sin I am,
>   Thou art full of truth and grace.

and add ' Amen ', as if perfectly satisfied that such an antithesis should remain without any atonement.

[1] Cp. my *Circumstances or Character?* (Methuen, 1911), *Free Dispensaries*, p. 91.

of principles of relief in our visitors, and on some uniformity of plan over the whole parish. We can work for a proper relief committee, and for a social work committee dealing with questions other than relief. We can organize collecting savings banks to give visitors, who want to do something and have no ideas beyond doles, a better and more useful outlet for their sympathies. We may work in all these directions for the separation of relief from religious profession.

The attitude of dependence.

But the work will still only be half done. We have to combat the general attitude of dependence on the vicar. He is, as things are now, expected to entertain, to give parties for ' his ' workers, suppers to ' his ' choir, to shake hands with them on all possible occasions, to thank them for singing, as if they sang to his glory, to express his gratitude to ' his ' Sunday School teachers for all they do for him, to present confirmation manuals, to head subscription lists, to subsidize treats, clubs, and mothers' meetings, to pay for all sorts of things out of his own pocket, and to give at every service. The bag is sometimes even handed to the curates when the collection is for the Assistant Clergy Fund !

To change this general attitude the wrong spirit must be attacked wherever it appears. The first step is in most cases to make clear the finances of the parish so that the people may at least know how much the vicar gives. There is, of course, no reason why he should not give like anybody else, but the sums given should pass through the accounts and figure on each side, as receipts and expenditure. Then we may begin to work steadily all round for independence. The children who have treats should be made to save up some of the cost ; when the cost is met by their contributions and those of their parents they should begin to contribute for the fares also. As soon as the mothers' meetings are self-supporting they may aim, as is customary in the North of England, at getting up teas and entertainments, selling the tickets and raising something for the church funds. It should be suggested to the god-parents that they are the right people to give manuals to their god-children at the Confirmation. A petty cash fund should be created to pay for postage and other expenses incidental to parish management which now generally fall on the vicar. The people should get to see that it is their place to entertain the clergy rather than that of the clergy to entertain them, and that this duty is not fulfilled merely by the making of Easter offerings. The support of the whole clergy should be the obligation of the laity. There is little doubt that as soon as they began to regard the Church as a body not to do things for them, but as one to be served with the same loyalty and devotion as their country, there would be far more reality in their religion.

IV

So far we have confined our attention to the co-ordination of forces within the parish. We shall consider the question of combining the forces of different parishes for larger aims in another chapter. But even in matters purely parochial one parish can help another.

At present there is a great waste of energy. Is it quite certainly the ideal that in towns, for instance, there should be daily services in each church when all are sparsely attended ? Might it not be better for the parishes to combine and arrange a rota of week-day offices so that a really representative body of churchmen rendered the offices in the district, with a sense of corporate life extending beyond the mere parish ? On Sundays practically all churches have a celebration of the Eucharist at 8 a.m., but few or none at 8.15, at 8.30, or at 9 a.m. Yet devout people sometimes oversleep themselves, and obviously the more hours there are to choose from the easier it is for different members of one household to attend. Innumerable sermons and addresses are given in each church, for the most part by the same people and to the same hearers : surely labour might

Interparochialism.

Wasted energy.

be saved and the message better given by arranging systematic interchange of pulpits, so that it might be worth while to give considerable care in preparation to a sermon that would be preached several times. This is what is done in effect by University Extension lecturers with no loss to their sincerity, and with certain gain in interest to their work. In the work of propaganda, if a parish has too few readers to make it worth while starting a good church library, why should there not be circulating libraries and church magazine societies in the Archdeaconry ? The effect of bringing men of different schools of thought together, not to discuss differences but to unite in common work in which all agree, would surely be all to the good.

Influence of one parish on another. One parish would help another. At present each has to fight its own battles, and success in one hardly does anything to help the other. But with a wider outlook over the larger area of work we could always point to other parishes where the experiment that we want to make has proved successful. Where the thing is seen in concrete form it is easier to understand. It is always more convincing to show in working than to explain in words. So far this influence of parish on parish has been mainly exercised in matters of ceremonial. People have been ready to copy what they see in use elsewhere, but the same help might be found in matters of music, of children's services, of church arrangements, of vestry discipline, and of parish organization generally.

Again, abuses often go unchecked for personal reasons. The organist is incompetent, but ' he is such a good fellow '. ' He deafens us and makes the boys shout dreadfully ', but ' he has been there so many years '. It is impossible for the local people to act, but a diocesan Church Music Society could visit and advise with less offence. Or the vicar is careless about finance and it is difficult for any one to say anything. If the accounts had to be submitted to a diocesan auditor the matter would at once be rectified. The

choir is irreverent ; the men do not kneel and, if communicants, are obviously only so because there is a rule that they
must be. A new-comer cannot remedy the evil at once.
But if we had a system of commendation from choir to
choir, in time new men accustomed to a better tradition
could be found. Meanwhile, by united choir services the
best could set an example which would instinctively be
copied. By taking in and circulating a good choir paper
(if the right one could be found), by carrying on a correspondence in the musical Press, something could be done
towards forming a better public opinion. Shouting,
mechanical beating out of plain-song, vulgarity in hymn
singing, could be corrected by practising for a festival,
especially if the conductor were to attend local rehearsals.[1]
It is difficult to tell servers not to fuss and fidget ; still more
difficult to warn an individual sacristan against familiarity
with boy servers, but at a combined meeting of a guild of
servers, advice and warnings could be given quite imper-
sonally. The scandal of bell-ringers calling people to
church and walking away themselves will not be cured by
a rebuke, but the unseemliness of the bad tradition and its
naturalness if no provision is made for washing after ringing,
could be brought home to them and to the clergy who complain, at a bell-ringing festival or in the pages of the *Bell
News.*

V

The remedy is the same as that which has transformed
industry. We must learn to take a wider view in our work,
to carry more ideas in our mind at a time, to have plans of
a larger scope, with more elements co-operating in their
working. We must learn to make one part work in with
another, an influence here back up an effort there.

Need of a wider out-look.

If we are to do this we must learn to work not only in
co-operation but also in consultation with one another. We

Working by Com-mittees.

[1] What the Welsh people have done for hymn singing by their ' Cyman-
faoedd Ganu ' is well known.

must adopt the same kind of method of working by councils and committees that is found necessary in all other departments of life. They do not (unless mismanaged) waste time. If they did, tiresome as they generally are, they would not be so universally adopted by all intelligent people. In the multitude of counsellors there has always been strength, and two heads are proverbially better than one. We must get rid of the popular prejudice against committees. It is mainly due to amateurishness and inexperience.[1]

Training in self-government.

It may be true that most parishes are not ready for such co-operative management, nor in our present state of inexperience is it easy to decide on exactly the right machinery. Moreover, the younger clergy and the unbeneficed cannot force incumbents to new methods, and still less can the laity do so. But all can begin working to the desired end. We can be educating church people in the idea of self-government. In clubs, in relief committees, in the choir, in the free-will offering scheme, we can see to it that nothing is allowed to be a ' one man show ', that our boys and girls are being trained in the forms and procedure of committee work, that our adults are being encouraged to apply to church government the same methods with which they are familiar in their business or municipal life. The next generation will then be ready to take up its responsibilities. It is a problem needing time for its solution, and needing, besides time, a co-ordination of many forces to effect the desired result.

[1] Cp. Walter Bagehot, *Literary Studies* (Longmans), 1907, vol. iii, p. 211 : ' Experience shows that no man is on all points so wise as the mass of men are after a good discussion.'

CHAPTER III

THE STANDARD OF WORK

'Ancora imparo.'—*Attributed to Michael Angelo.*

We have seen how the class divisions of society are bound up with the fact that men differ in their power of looking ahead, and how the industrial revolution has altered the nature of work in the factory and of life in the home, but beyond these changes in the external organization of social life there is another in the individual which is characteristic of to-day, namely, the change in his skill and in the personal character required or created. Skill and specialization.

The effect of modern conditions of life is, no doubt, sometimes bad. A man may spend his whole life in one job, or in a mere single process that needs no particular skill and evokes no particular interest. This is the side generally dwelt on by writers. But it is probably his own fault if he does so. Either he is not up to more, or he lacks initiative to push on. He gets left behind because others leave the particular work to him. Even such a man, however, gets a far better wage, and lives in far greater comfort, than he did when doing similar unintelligent mechanical work in days of old.

On the other hand, to the majority the external conditions of modern industrial life give an immense stimulus to efficiency. The man has to fit in with machinery which is efficient. He has to train himself to work in with elaborated schemes which must work punctually and exactly if they are to avoid confusion and disaster. It has been pointed out how the railways have produced a characteristic type of man in their guards, active, trustworthy, ready, punctual, and capable. Contact with other men sharpens the wits. Even the mere specialization on a detail of work, into which many drop down, produces a high standard of The stimulus of efficiency.

skill in one particular direction. The surroundings of work similarly influence many. The shopman has to be smart in appearance and to learn to deal with customers. The commercial traveller becomes used to a high standard of efficiency in the hotels he puts up at, in the papers he reads, in the music halls and picture palaces where he finds his amusement. The performances may be vulgar, the papers superficial, the hotels furnished in bad taste, but they are efficient. The work done is done thoroughly. So, from work and circumstances are forged characters in men strong out of proportion to their learning, to their intellectual powers, to their culture. It is often a shock to talk to some of the well-set-up, well-appointed, men who might have stepped out of one of Mr. Arnold Bennett's novels, so inferior are their ideas to their appearance, but they are vigorous, capable, and forcible. If they have not acquired the ' music of speech ' they are able to do every kind of service smartly and neatly[1], and—the fact significant to what we are considering—they are accustomed everywhere in their world to efficiency. Moreover, from the great mobility of modern society has come an enormous increase of openings. The world is no longer an oyster ; it is rather an orchard with fruit trees asking to be robbed of their fruit, though perhaps the best hangs from the upper branches, difficult to get at and not always easy even to see. The versatile man passes from one task to another, and rises rapidly if they are strung together on a definite purpose and if he knows how to use his experience. This leads to continual differentiation of skill and to specialization in the higher branches of industry. There is always room at the top, and the increased interest men find in the best work again leads to still greater efficiency. These specialists again focus their activities in societies and their learning in publications. Trade papers and conferences carry knowledge abroad and test experience at home. It is found worth while to set

Increase of opportunity.

[1] Plato, *Theaetetus*, 176.

aside certain men as students to devote their time to research and speculation in order to further the interests of the whole body and continually to raise the standard of work.

Advance depends on the span and area of work, but still more on versatility, on mobility of labour, on seeing relationships and grasping opportunities, on specialization, on pioneer activity opening up new branches of work. With all this goes increased self-respect, self-confidence, and mental power. How is the case with the Church ?

I

It is generally admitted that the standard of clerical work is low. The Report of the Committee of Convocation issued in 1908 [1] only echoes the complaint that has rung out through centuries without being met.[2] It is only what we

Low standard of clerical work.

---

[1] *The Supply and Training of Candidates for Holy Orders.* Report with notes, appendices, and recommendations presented to the Archbishop of Canterbury by the Committee appointed by His Grace, at the request of the Bishops of the Provinces of Canterbury and York, to consider the question of the supply and training of candidates for the Sacred Ministry. June 1908. S.P.C.K.

[2] E. g. ' Cum in rebus frivolis tam sumus solliciti, tamen ad Ecclesiasticae munus audet aliquis accedere, nihilo maius instructus quam arator ad citharam, nauta ad aratrum ; proque tot eximiis virtutibus, quas officii postulat dignitas, nihil affert praeter perfrictam egregie frontem et impudentiam,' Erasmus, *Eccles.*, p. 81. Quoted in J. J. Van Oosterzee, *Practical Theology*, Eng. Tr. (Hodder & Stoughton), 1878, p. 45. Cp. also Hooker, *Eccles. Polity*, Bk. V, ch. xxxi ; Barnabas Oley's introduction to George Herbert's *Priest to the Temple* in *The Clergyman's Instructor*, 4th ed. (Oxford), 1837, p. 10. Pepys's *Diary*, February 1668 : ' Much discourse about the bad state of the Church, and how the clergy are come to be men of no worth in the world, and as the world do now generally discourse they must be reformed'. Burnett, *History of the Reformation*, author's abridged edition (Gibbings), 1903, p. 145 : ' The want of such houses for the strict education of those who are to serve in the Church has been the occasion of many fatal consequences since that time, by the scandals which men initiated into the sacred functions before they were well prepared for them have given to the world'. Cp. also Bingham, *Antiquities*, Bk. VI, ch. v, §§ 5–8.

should expect if we compare the training given to the clergy with that which gives an artisan his trade, prepares a teacher for his profession, or qualifies a doctor to practise. For a man educated at a university, one year at a theological college for theological study and its special application to clerical work, is all that is now given, and two years if education, theological knowledge, and practical training are all necessary.

No school of training.

In many departments of life training is got after a man has begun his work. Useful as are technical schools, the artisan's chief training is given in his shop. An Officer's Training Corps at school or college can do valuable work, but an officer learns most of his business in the Army itself. The doctor does not learn by lectures alone ; the hospitals form the more important training ground. The social worker reads and attends lectures, but practical work is learned at Settlements and in Charity Organization offices. But the clergy have practically no school of training corresponding to the shop where efficient work is in full swing, no system of graded responsibility as have the officers in the Army, no body of work built up on experienced tradition as in the hospital or C.O.S. Office, with all the opportunities for specialization that they afford. At best the parish can train him during his diaconate in very elementary matters. Each priest's work is practically the same in its externals, to which he has to conform, and in its limitations in the things he is not allowed to do. There is no one clear conception of his calling to give a unity of ideal that would admit of free development into varieties of practice. Each man is expected to do all the different parts of the work, so there can be little differentiation in the work itself. Each member of the staff is perhaps ' given a district ' instead of being entrusted with an interest, regardless of the fact that modern society is linked together by interests, and that you cannot confine human relationships to a set area arbitrarily marked off. It may be good as an apprenticeship to go through all the different parts of the work, and a first curacy may, perhaps, be better sought in a country town, where all classes have to be dealt with and all the parishioners and their interests are known. A draper who has gone through the shop and learned all the departments of the trade in the provinces, has advantages when he comes up to specialize in a London wholesale warehouse, but in the Church there is no real opportunity for specialization. There are superficial and violent variations, both in teaching and in ceremonial, but in method the same type, and towards work the same attitude, prevails in practically all parishes.

This does not make for efficiency, and is all the more fatal to a high standard of work because circumstances react on character. The clergy are ridiculed on the Stage, and in *Punch*, to say nothing of the ' comic ' and hostile press. Their present surroundings tend to make them slovenly as those of the commercial traveller tend to make him smart. This is, no doubt, a superficial matter, but it is an index of inner effectiveness. It alienates men accustomed to efficiency in their shops, hotels, and papers. If they find it in theatres they expect it in church, and failing to find a religion that can enter into their lives, their smartness degenerates into vulgarity and indecency. Moreover, this inefficiency of clerical life and work deters men from seeking Holy Orders. Others, after ordination, slip out, some to Rome, others quietly into lay life—and these are more in number than perhaps most of us are aware of. *The effect on character.*

II

Efficiency follows when work is continuous and unified. The worker improves by experience, and his fellow workers keep him up to the mark. This experience must first be gained on the basis of ordinary normal work, by the parson, that is, in that of the parish. He must serve his apprenticeship first as a student and then as a worker. *Efficiency and training.*

I have dealt elsewhere with the training of the student of

Pastoral Theology.[1] The right discipline should produce men devout, natural, alert, punctual, with sufficient teaching and preaching power, ready to see and to form sound judgements on all that comes under their notice. But more than this is wanted. The work begun at the theological college should be continued through the whole of after life. Here, however, we are met with an obstacle in the position of the unbeneficed clergy.

The unbeneficed.

At present a young curate is allowed far too much liberty and given far too little freedom. He is allowed not to do things but is prevented from doing them. His discipline is all negative. He is suffered, if he wishes, to be slack. The majority of vicars are far too kind, and it is a very bad thing for those under them. On the other hand the curate has practically no guidance, nor does he always feel that his vicar is qualified to guide. His authority seems to consist chiefly in ' telling him he mustn't '. The curate is given no responsibility and has no status, either at the beginning of his career or after twenty years' service. Though it is a commonplace of all training that you must give responsibility to students, even at the risk of the work not being so well done, and that no one will continue to work his best unless he can gain some sort of recognized position by good work, the curate is seldom allowed to do anything on his own initiative, seldom suffered to feel his feet. The pleasant personal relationships generally existing between him and his vicar make professional relationships all the harder ; every suggestion that he makes becomes a criticism, and every criticism a complaint. Differences of opinion are felt to be rude. Imaginary grievances are kept silent and nursed. For real grievances there is no redress.

Closer relation to the bishop needed

The matter is a difficult one, but the first need seems to be that of a more direct relation to the bishop, and—since finance is at the bottom of most questions—of direct pay-

[1] *An Introduction to the Study of Pastoral Theology* (Oxford), 1912, Bk. II, ch. ii.

ment of salary from diocesan sources. This is not merely necessary to insure an income increasing with length of service (no small point in itself), or to avoid trouble between vicar and curate ; we are thinking rather of the need of efficiency. If salaries were drawn from a diocesan source, the bishop could see that each deacon was properly trained. He could prevent hard-worked or unscrupulous incumbents exploiting them. He could make it impossible that any young man should have to preach one hundred and forty-seven sermons in the first year after his ordination.[1]

The feeling that some one knows, and presumably cares, what you are doing is a great stimulus to good work. A dossier of each priest in the diocese should be kept, if only that the consciousness that there was some such record might give continuity and aim to work. It is not generally recognized how depressing it is to the ordinary man to feel that no one in authority in the least knows what he is doing. There should be opportunities for those who seek more responsible work to qualify themselves for it. Training in the art of teaching, in social work, in mission or open-air preaching, in music, should be available. Summer schools of study should be arranged, and any qualifications gained should be registered in each man's record. He should be able to move to another parish or diocese without losing status. He should have, not merely a security of livelihood and of an increasing salary, but chance of a career, scope for a legitimate ambition to serve in higher branches of his work, opportunities of qualifying for greater responsibility and recognition, for, as Bias of Priene said, ' office shows the man ' [2]. *Need of opportunities for a career.*

A higher standard of work would at once lead to the delegation of much routine work and detail to others. Letters could be written, accounts kept, and visits paid, by lay workers occupying the same position in the parish as *Delegation of work.*

---

[1] As had a young deacon of my acquaintance.

[2] Ἀρχὴ ἄνδρα δείξει, in Aristotle, *Eth. Nic.*, Bk. V, ch. i, § 16.

that of clerks in an office. This would soon improve the position of lay workers as well, for they would also have a recognized status and definite work for which they too could be specially trained. They would become a regular part of the Church's system. They would become necessary and indispensable, and would so have a future secured to them and be set free from the haunting fear of being turned adrift in their old age. Much good work is already being attempted in this direction, especially for the training of women workers, but the results will not be nearly so great as they might be if the clergy who are to be over them remain amateurish and untrained in their calling.[1]

Leading to real knowledge.

Utilizing the work and experience of others gives a wider area for generalization, and removes the danger of personal error and individual prejudice. The clergy, when working through an organized staff, would soon be able really to know their people in a way that is impossible by merely scurrying round the parish. More than that ; they would realize that each parish was part of a larger whole and would get to know their district, to understand its character,

[1] Cp. a Report to the Southwark Diocesan Conference, 1914, presented by a Committee on the Status of the Unbeneficed Clergy which passed the following resolutions : (1)' That during the first five years immediately after Ordination the spiritual, intellectual, and pastoral training of every Deacon and Priest should be inquired into annually, and as far as possible supplemented by Episcopal authority.'

(2) ' That on the recommendation of the Bishop an Assistant Priest who has served seven years in the Diocese should receive, in addition to his stipend parochial—calculated for this purpose as £160 per annum— an increment of £10 a year, to be paid from a Diocesan Fund, up to £180 if single, and if married up to £220 ; and that this resolution be referred to the Committee of Diocesan Finance.'

(3) ' That, seeing that the Church should be responsible for those she ordains, a man who at the avoidance of a benefice falls out of employment, should be offered employment in the same diocese where at that time he was at work, with not less than the same remuneration.'

(4) ' That the Bishop be requested to appoint an Advisory Board to assist him in all matters connected with the Assistant Clergy, from which Board he could, for example, select assessors to advise him in the case of an appeal of an Assistant Curate against dismissal by an Incumbent.'

and to appreciate its thought.   They would get a real knowledge of its social and spiritual conditions, of the relations
in it of rich and poor and, more important still, of the classes
in between.   They would get to know why one district is
different from another, what were the mutual relationships
of one element with another, what the influence of ideas
dominant or losing their force.

With increased efficiency and with the corresponding
power of reckoning with all the different strands of the
varied life of men, would come the evolution of experts.
Just as in social work, after a general training, one worker will
specialize with children, another with the hospitals, another
will be found to have gifts for rescue work, another for
Poor Law administration, so the clergy could develop their
peculiar powers and gifts in their calling.   We sorely need
men who will devote particular attention to the problems of
religious education in secondary and public schools and at
the universities, and not merely to those in elementary
schools.   Others might be called to specialize with reference
to sickness, finding out what are really the best methods of
dealing with the sick, studying the psychology of ill-health,
investigating the action of religion and medicine as causes
of cure.   Others might make a special study of the work of
the Church under the Poor Law, to find out how to serve
paupers in spite of the opposition of intolerant Guardians,
how to set up the right connexion between religious influence within the House and outside, how to meet the needs
of that isolated class of Poor Law officials who are charged
with such difficult and depressing duties.   The work of
chaplains with prisoners needs special gifts which are not
always possessed by the clergy appointed, as readers of
Lady Constance Lytton's *Prisons and Prisoners* will have
realized.   The whole work of open air apologetics[1] needs

The creation of experts.

[1] The un- or inter-denominational Christian Evidence Society (37
Craven Street, Strand) is taking this work in hand, and is always in
great need of help both in money and of speakers, but the Church ought
to be doing the work herself.

a special class of workers, not merely because it requires time and energy which the parish priest can hardly spare, but also because its various methods, their effectiveness apparent and real, and their justification, need to be carefully studied, so that a body of tested experience may be available for those new to the work, or as a step to further developments. The literary propaganda of Christianity, both by popular leaflets and tracts and by letters and articles in the press, is at present only effectively done by certain societies and publishing houses, while the problem of distribution as a definite missionary and religious effort is hardly touched.

Expert knowledge.

Such experts might then confer to the immense furthering of our knowledge. Conferences of people with special experience are as profitable and useful as a meeting got up because a meeting is due is tiresome and dull. Such experiences gained in various centres might be pooled as, for instance, that of workers in the Mothers' Union in the Church, or those of Co-operators, of Trade Unions, or of teachers outside, is collected by periodical gatherings. In this way many mistakes might be rectified; mistakes in method such as that of the amateur Christian Evidence worker who interrupts the secularist speaker and so gives him the opportunity he is looking for, mistakes in music maintained by tradition, mistakes in architecture found out only when the church has been built. Untried assertions, those frequent sources of hindrance might be pricked; instead of repeating *a priori* assumptions, such as that it is ' dogma that keeps men from church ', or that ' theological colleges are narrowing ', or that ' the poor ' like this or that, we might find out what really ' puts people off ' from religion, what are the defects in our training of the clergy, and what is common to all classes and what peculiar to some.

Help from fellow-workers.

In this much help could be got from the analogy of other work and of different callings. Perhaps the most obvious of these and the most directly fruitful, would be the field of foreign missions. No one can read our best mission litera- ture of to-day, such as, for example, the magazine *The East and the West*,[1] without being struck by the excellence of its tone and its capable attitude in the face of its problems. Its readiness to reckon with the facts and to see things as they are is the foundation of its good work. No less is it built up on a caution and an anxiety to utilize the experi- ence of others which make its whole attitude scientific and stamps it with some quality that gives an indefinable sense of satisfaction in contrast with much that we are familiar with at home. Yet many of our problems are extraordin- arily similar, and will, perhaps, be solved for us by workers thousands of miles away. The danger of basing Chris- tianity on expectation of benefits—of ' Rice Christianity '— is realized there in a way we fail to realize it at home. People who see clear issues abroad are often unable to recognize them in England. Many of the same men who at the Student Christian Conference at Liverpool in January 1912 [2] thought that they had secured unity by saying the Apostles' Creed together, each giving it a different inter- pretation, who at any rate made no protest against the disendowment of the Church in Wales, or against the political Nonconformist policy of thwarting church schools, loudly cheered their leader, Mr. Mott, a few weeks after at the Queen's Hall, when he pointed out that the three chief hindrances to Christianity on the Mission field were syncre- tism, the need of money, and lack of schools ! The various problems of Prayer Book reform and of elasticity of worship, which at home remain controversial and academic, are like to be settled, it would seem, by the natural genius of various races, Indian, Chinese, Japanese, Corean, each following its

[1] Published quarterly by the Society for the Propagation of the Gospel, Tufton Street, Westminster, S. W.

[2] A report of the Conference was published by the Student Volunteer Missionary Union (' Annandale,' North End Road, Golders Green, London, N.W.), under the title *Christ and Human Need*.

own religious instincts, even if guided by the longer experience of English Christianity.

Counter-acting party feeling.

Such conferences of experts as we have considered above would cut across the lines of party grouping in the Church. Those who were skilled in different kinds of work would be of all schools, ' High ', ' Low ', and ' Broad '. Such ' mutual conversations between persons of different persuasions ' would be found to have ' mollified those distempers and abated those sharpnesses, and extinguished those jealousies which make men unfit ' for taking counsel together.[1] It is sometimes said that theological colleges ' make men much less Low Church ' or ' send men out who came as High Churchmen much broader ' ; the experience of those who have to do with them is rather that the crudity of thought and amateurishness of outlook in students is cured by study and intercourse with other men while they remain just as keenly evangelical in spirit, or that what was at first over-external and superficial sinks down, owing to the same influences, into the character and heart.

Inter-denominational conferences have their peculiar value just because of the differences between those who take part in them, and become possible only when it is fully realized that co-operation in religious work is impossible because of those differences. Churchmen should take every opportunity of furthering such, not only when on social and other questions in which differences do not come in, but on directly religious matters, so that each may learn to understand and respect the opinions of others much as he may disagree with them. Similarly, sympathetic intercourse with atheists at home, or with the heathen abroad, either informal or formal, seems an almost necessary condition of the truth (as we hold it to be) being accepted by them.

[1] E. Cardwell, *A History of Conferences connected with the Revision of the Book of Common Prayer* (Oxford), 1840, p. 296. King Charles's ' Declaration to all his loving subjects of his Kingdom of England and Dominion of Wales concerning Ecclesiastical affairs '.

A higher standard of clerical work would make easier an approach to secular bodies and persons whose interests in life are not primarily ecclesiastical, for the clergy would meet them on the common ground of efficiency. A man who knows his work has always much less difficulty in understanding and appreciating the work of others. The bar between clerical and lay thought will not be removed by the clergy trying to pose as laymen, but by each being recognized as knowing his own business. This would be of mutual service between different professions. Artists would be the better for the inspiration of Christianity, and our churches would be spared much disfigurement if handicraft and priestcraft were on the same level of skill and could interchange their special knowledge. Ecclesiastical furnishing shops would disappear and religious *objets de piété* and church furniture would be wrought in the best studios. Instead of spending our chief energies in Sunday School reform we should be co-operating with religious men in the educational world in securing a place for Christian schooling in our national system of education. Instead of relying on organizers and inspectors who are of the clergy first and of the school world only incidentally, we should be able to use the services of Christian teachers and professors who have expert knowledge of education. The Moral Education League has unfortunately subordinated its aims to those of general secularist propaganda. When, yielding to the advice of men who knew what education means, it changed its policy and gathered together in conference all those interested in moral training even if they were Christians, it produced two excellent volumes of permanent value and did a really useful piece of work by its Congress.[1]

Co-operation with laymen.

[1] *Moral Instruction and Training in Schools.* Report of an International Inquiry. Edited on behalf of the Committee by M. E. Sadler (Longmans), 1908. *Papers on Moral Education communicated to the first International Moral Education Congress held at the University of London,* September 25–29, edited by Gustav Spiller (David Nutt), 1908.

III

Increased dignity of clerical work.

If the clergyman's work could be thus brought into line with the work of other men, the work itself would be done with greater interest and more self-respect. It would be obviously work worthy of a man and many more would be attracted to apply as candidates for Holy Orders. There would no longer be grumbling about committee meetings as waste of time, or refusal to fill up forms as mere machinery, as no doubt at present they often are. If it were the case that a proper agenda was prepared for the meetings and the secretary's orders were carried out, the use of them would be seen at once. As soon as there was a demand for accurate information on important subjects no one would object to the detailed work of collecting that information. At any rate, no one would grumble more than does every Englishman who yet knows how to do his work. Many other disagreeable and tiresome things which are now neglected as obviously useless would be done, if not with alacrity at least with patience if it were recognized that they led to something larger and more important.

Office organization.

For such a raising of the standard of work it seems almost a necessity that some organization more nearly approaching that of an office in ordinary business must be set up in our parishes, and something more nearly approaching office hours kept. The clergy, no doubt, work for long hours with little relief, and much of their duty is so diffused that it cannot be confined to a working day of six or eight hours. But it cannot be denied that this fact also gives easy opportunity for wasting time, and that the lack of clearly-defined hours makes it difficult for the laity to judge them by the same standard as that by which they judge themselves. There is little doubt that the common experience of men that harder work is done in the regular surroundings of an office, factory, or studio, applies equally to men whose calling is that of a priest.

Our great need is of effective thought and of a clergy who are continually advancing in experience. ' In a Government office,' writes Mr. Graham Wallas, ' as certainly as in a law court or laboratory, effective thinking will not be done unless adequate opportunities are secured by organization during the whole working life of the appointed officials.' [1] To the law court, laboratory, and Government office we may add the Church. ' In at least one office ', he goes on to tell us, ' the important papers are brought first to the chief. His decision is at once given and is sent down the hierarchy for elaboration. In other offices the younger men are given invaluable experience, and the elder men are prevented from getting into an official rut, by a system which requires that all papers should be sent first to a junior, who sends them up to his senior accompanied not only by the necessary papers but also by a minute of his own suggesting official action.' But in the Church we still mainly rely on the methods of Moses before he met again his sensible father-in-law Jethro.[2]

Growth in experience.

Mr. Graham Wallas goes on to point out how in one Government department a deliberate policy has been adopted of training junior officials by transferring them at regular intervals to different branches of the work, to recommend that clerks in another should at least once in their career become personally acquainted with work in different parts of the country, and to suggest that there should be ' definite periods of study, during which an official on leave of absence, with full pay, should acquire some knowledge useful to his department, after which he should show the result of his work, not by the answering of examination questions but by the presentation of a book or report of permanent value.' With a sound system of finance it would not be impossible for the Church to adopt similar methods, sending country men to visit town parishes and vice versa, giving a man who has been seven years in one

Training of junior officials.

[1] *Human Nature in Politics*, p. 261.   [2] Exodus xviii. 13–27.

place six or twelve months to visit a mission field, or setting the more practical a similar period of specialized work, sending them round with archdeacons on a tour of systematic inspection and reporting, or setting free the more studious for reading or writing at one of the Universities or Libraries of England, Switzerland, or America.[1]

Harm of disorganization.

But this is not likely to come to pass just yet. The need for such a change in our methods is little recognized by the mass of the clergy, and perhaps least of all by their leaders. They are older men who have grown up under present conditions. Many still decry organization, in spite of the terrible lessons of the war, and advise more house to house visiting as a panacea for all ills. As is always the case in a badly-managed office, so in the Church the chiefs are overwhelmed with work. They have far more than they can do, and do not realize the waste of energy among the rank and file of the clergy who are kept busy with trivial matters. The younger clergy must be the pioneers. The necessary machinery is not likely to be created for them, so they should set about creating it for themselves. They should organize a system of voluntary mutual inspection. Criticism and comment is not resented when made according to the rules of the game, as any one who has been coached in rowing readily understands. Much of the gathering of experience on general and special subjects that we have desiderated could be done on such a voluntary basis. If freedom of action and initiative is checked in work, at least thoughts are free, and we are at liberty to create new ideals. If official conferences and pooling of experience does not exist, much could be done to prepare the way for them by

[1] It will hardly be possible in this generation for German universities to be used in this manner. In France, unfortunately, the Government has been deliberately hostile to the Church; whilst in Holland, Denmark, Norway, Sweden, and Russia, the language would be a bar to most students. In England St. Deiniol's Library at Hawarden, where this chapter was written, affords exceptional opportunities for theological study.

junior clerical societies. If the training of the clergy is insufficient, self-training, if harder, is perhaps more effective. If the standard of work is to be raised, there is, after all, no better way of raising it than by each steadily determining to make himself more efficient. When all is said, that is the way men rise and manufacture improves in the industrial world, and that is at least one way in which younger men can get more opportunity and raise the whole standard of clerical work.

CHAPTER IV

POLICY IN WORK

'Ο δὲ μὴ δυνάμενος κοινωνεῖν ἢ μηθὲν δεόμενος δι' αὐτάρκειαν οὐθὲν μέρος πόλεως, ὥστε ἢ θηρίον ἢ θεός, Aristotle, *Polit.* i. 2, § 48.

Industrial-ism and the upper classes.

WE have noted the change in modern social conditions in three particulars—in time, in extent, and in the matter of specialization ; and we have tried to find out some of the corresponding changes needed in Pastoral Theology, in the span of sustained work, in the area of co-operative effort, and in the standard of efficiency attained by the clergy. In examining the change of industrial conditions and methods we naturally think first of the effect on the particular work and on the ordinary worker ; so in considering the parallel change in church life we have so far limited our view to the parish and the parish clergy. But the effect of the economic change of recent generations has been increasingly marked as we ascend in the social scale, and is greatest in the highest or governing classes. In what does this change consist ?

I

Domestic life.

The older social structure was primarily domestic. It centred in the home where, we may suppose, the mother reigned supreme. It involved the education of the children in the family by father and mother. It was supported by the agriculture or handicraft which was carried on under the direction of the father in his surrounding plot of land, or as a domestic industry. Local affairs were settled by heads of families who all knew one another. All was direct and managed under personal observation.

The basis of Society.

Such domestic life is the basis of all human society. It survives still in the permanent institution of the family, and admits of a considerable degree of adaptation to other and larger areas. Thus a capable woman will carry on a large boarding-house on the model of a home and give personal attention to her guests. An expert caterer will expand the home dinner-table to the array of a large restaurant and feed even hundreds of customers at once, getting to know their tastes and preferences as a mother does those of her children. Similarly, by the artificial discipline of a school, the schoolmaster can extend the parental relationship in teaching to a class of thirty, or even fifty, boys, but having to deal with more than one appetite his numbers must be smaller than those of the caterer. By specializing and confining his attention solely to management the head master or principal can effectively guide a larger number. By the organization of industry a foreman can look after a gang of men, and a manager direct even hundreds in a factory.

But the essence of all such management is that there should be direct personal supervision by an individual, and the powers of any individual are limited. As Aristotle saw, though man is a political animal and cannot live alone, we cannot really know more than a few out of all the men in the world.[1]

---

[1] *Eth. Nic.*, Bk. I, ch. v (vii), vi : ' When we speak of self-sufficiency, we do not mean that a person leads a solitary life all by himself, but that he has parents, children, wife, and friends, and fellow-citizens in general, as man is naturally a social being. But here it is necessary to prescribe some limit ; for if the circle be extended so as to include parents, descendants, and friends' friends, it will go on indefinitely.'

Bk. IX, ch. x, § 3 : ' Is there a fixed limitation to the size of a circle of friends as there is to the size of a state ? For ten people would not be enough to compose a state ; on the other hand, if the population rose to a hundred thousand, it would cease to be a state. It may be suggested, however, that the number of citizens is not a single fixed amount, but may be anything within certain definite limits. So, too, there will be a definite limit to the number of friends. It will be, I think, the highest number with whom a person could live. For it is community of life which we saw to be the especial characteristic of friendship, and it is easy to see that a person cannot live with a number of people and distribute himself among them.'

Cp. Jeremy Taylor, *A Discourse of the Nature, Offices and Measures of*

It is impossible to share the same pleasures with a great number. We must seek, not as many friends as possible, but as many as make society. The natural limit is set by the size of the family and immediate friends. If we attempt to extend this limit unduly ' it goes off into indefiniteness ' (εἰς ἄπειρον).

So in a school, with classes larger than thirty the thoroughness of the teaching grows less.[1] There is a general opinion that if a training college much exceeds the same number its character alters. A factory can be supervised, but not a whole business. As a logical outcome of the same conception of the necessity of personal knowledge which underlay the Greek conception of the city state, Aristotle declared that cities must not be too big. Very populous cities were, he said, rarely well grounded. There was a limit to the size of states as there was to other things, to implements or ships—a ship a span long would not be a ship nor would one that was a quarter of a mile long. A city of ten would not be a city, neither would one of a hundred thousand. Babylon was a nation, not a state. Such a state, he declared, would want a herald with a voice of thunder. If citizens were to distribute office according to merit they would have to know the people's characters. ' Clearly, then, the best

Friendship, Works, vol. xi, p. 305 : ' The universal friendship of which I speak must be limited because we are so. It must therefore follow that our friendships to mankind may admit variety as does our conversation ; and as by nature we are made sociable to all, so we are friendly ; but as all cannot actually be of our society, so neither can all be admitted to a special actual friendship.'

[1] *Life and Letters of Edward Thring*, G. R. Parkin (Macmillan), 2nd ed., ch. iv, pp. 71–4. Writing in 1859 he says : ' There are no principles more definite than the principles which determine that an efficient school must not pass certain boundaries in the matter of numbers.' The numbers he gives are : for a house, 30 ; for a class, 20–25 ; for a school, 330. Cp. also J. J. Findlay, *Principles of Class Teaching* (Macmillan's Manuals for Teachers), 1911, p. 13 : ' We may, I think, take it as a common opinion that a teacher of experience will usually be willing to handle a class of thirty pupils, if the thirty are fairly equal in attainments ; he would be unwilling to go up to forty, or to fall below twenty.'

limit of the population is the largest number which suffices
for the purpose of life and can be taken in at a single view.' [1]
As Plato said, ' There is no greater good in the State than
that the citizens should be known to one another.' [2] Cannot
we hear the echo of this to-day—' The ideal parish is one
large enough to call forth a man's best energies, but not too
large to prevent the vicar from becoming personally acquainted with every member of his flock and making them
know one another ' ?

But, as a matter of fact, the martyred *Lusitania* was
nearly a quarter of a mile long. Implements are no longer
limited to hand-driven machines, but are elaborated into
the plant of factories. The ideal of the Greek city state,
even though it could command the labour of unenfranchised
slaves, was a failure when applied to the conditions of the
Roman Empire, and a fruitful source of confusion and
tyranny in later times, just as our transference of feudal and
country methods of church work to town conditions has
proved to-day.[3] For as industry has developed its leaders
have learned to work from an office and by abstractions.
They know how to deal with facts by reports and figures,
to judge men by testimonials and records, and they have
found that this is a surer method of dealing with them and
judging them than that actual inspection which is so apt to
be misled by externals. They have discovered how to carry
on trade by joint stock companies, which employ secretaries
and are directed by boards. They have learned not to confine their attention to facts and objects, but to deal with
movements, to consider markets, to anticipate fashions, to
reckon with human nature in advertisement, and to exercise
their imagination in laying plans and making discoveries.
Qui facit per alium facit per se. We have come to see that

*And go-
vernment.*

---

[1] *Politics*, Bk. VII, ch. iv, vii, ix, xi, and Bk. III, ch. iii, v, xii, xiii, xiv.
[2] *Laws*, Bk. V. 738.
[3] Cp. my *Circumstances or Character ? The Origins of Modern Church
Work*, pp. 59 ff.

administration counts for more than hard work, that mind is more than matter, and that faith is more than sight.[1] In other words, management has become government, for management is limited to the directing of what is under the eye, while the essence of government is that it works through others, by abstractions, with all the greater mental and moral power thereby evoked.

Women and men.

Now it may be noticed that by nature, training, and tradition women make better managers. In the sphere of the home common to both sexes, they play a greater part if only because of the fact of motherhood. They have for the same reason a greater interest in teaching and, for the young at least, make better teachers. The practice of the lesser arts and handicrafts still comes more natural to them. But men make better governors by their nature, their work, and their traditions. The necessity of earning drives them out of doors. The man who pushes out into the larger world succeeds. Interest in politics is natural to them as they have to exercise their imagination and take a wider, if sometimes less practical, view. Both elements—the care for detail and the power of initiative—are necessary for any healthy society. If in an institution one sex predominates, the characteristics of that sex become prominent. Women are better at management ; men at government. Women form the majority of active members of the Church of

---

[1] Cp. H. Withers, *Poverty and Waste* (Smith Elder), 1914, p. 74: 'Success in an industry in these days depends much more on good organization and skill in the purchase of raw material and judgement in the sale of the finished product than on the efficiency of the workers, important though that still is. This is a fact that is often forgotten by those who are somewhat hasty in their claims on behalf of labour. It does not help the cause of labour to tell it that it ought to have more than there is for it, or to assume that because a certain number of men have worked for a given number of hours on a certain task, therefore the finished product must be worth so many pounds, and that therefore labour is entitled to that amount, less interest on capital. The world would be a much easier and pleasanter place to live in if these things were true, but they are quite untrue. It is not enough to work on a thing to give it value.'

England, and she fails correspondingly in power of government.

Again, it must be realized that management and government are both personal functions. The former, however, is individual in its methods and is exercised chiefly on individuals. It gains force from directness, getting hold of people, and utilizing them as instruments and as channels to carry farther the original individual power. But its influence is limited by its qualities. Government, on the other hand, aims at influencing groups of persons, at diffusing ideas, and at originating movements. It works best in co-operation with others. It aims at leaving their personalities free, at stimulating their activities, at influencing fresh centres of spontaneous life. It is far *more* personal in that it demands the exercise of all the varied elements of personality, and is immensely more important in its effects, both in the matters it deals with and in the range of what it touches.

Management and government both personal.

II

Now it is a characteristic feature of English church life that we lay great stress on personal work. References to ' the all-important need of personal influence ', assertions that ' it is not organization but personality that tells ', or statements that ' however perfect our machinery, it cannot take the place of personal dealing ', meet with an immediate response of applause from the gallery. At the same time, we are continually lamenting our weakness. We are for ever complaining of popular indifference. And it is an undoubted fact that many men of the type the Church most needs do not respond to the call of Holy Orders. Have the two facts anything to do with one another ?

Personal work.

He would clearly be a foolish person who denied the power of personality. It tells in every branch of life. That goes without saying. On character depends the power of leadership, of initiative, of government. In the school, in the army, in business, it is the man that tells. But it is not this

Confused with individual work.

conception of personality that prompts our ideals of church work. We have confused ' personal ' work with ' individual' work. ' An individual ', write the authors of *The King's English*, ' is not simply a person, it is a single, separate, or private person, a person as opposed to a combination of persons.' To confuse the two, ' stamps a writer more definitely than almost any other single solecism, not as being generally ignorant or foolish, but as being without the literary sense.' [1] In practical life to confuse the two, as we have done, also stamps practical work with its peculiar mark. For the great mass of our parish work is of this kind. It consists of visiting, shaking hands, entertaining, exhorting, counting communicants and looking them up, pottering about in clubs for boys (who ought to be in a scouts' corps out with their scoutmaster), and trying to ' get hold of them', with much talk about ' my ' church, ' my ' parish, and ' my ' workers,[2] of thanking people who ' kindly ' arrange flowers for the altar, and choirmen for giving ' us ' such a delightful and bright service, and expressing our ' gratitude (*sic*) to our dear fellow-workers ' for all that they do. The predominant note of the whole is purely individual.

A higher type resented.

Not only so, but a higher type is resented. We decry organization—or did before the war. We grumble at having to fill in forms, and often refuse to do so even when stamped addressed envelopes for their return are enclosed.[3] We tell

[1] *The King's English* (Oxford), 1908, 2nd ed., pp. 53-6.

[2] I have even seen a letter in which the writer spoke of ' my ' Communion Service.

[3] The Secretary of the Special Committee appointed by the Bishop of London to obtain information from the clergy for the use of the Royal Poor Law Commission sent out, with a covering letter from the Bishop, a list of questions printed with spaces for replies and accompanied by a stamped addressed envelope, to the 570 beneficed clergy of the Diocese. Of these only about half replied. A second letter brought in replies from about one hundred more, but in the end replies were only obtained from about 400, a little over two-thirds of the whole number. The following extract from a Diocesan report on Sunday Schools tells the same tale. ' The fact that more than half the Incumbents have ignored

one another stories of men who skip committees for ' my visiting ' with evident approval. Yet in every other department of life, and in every grade of masculine work above the ranks of unskilled labour and minor retail trade (and perhaps that of the general practitioner), records are found necessary, and leading men work by boards and councils.

Let us look at some of the results of this ideal and of the methods it inspires. In the first place it necessarily limits our force to the power of one man. This, no doubt, is often considerable, especially in the case of younger men. But it rapidly tends to exhaustion. The strain of perpetual starting, when there is little continuity of purpose wears them out. Their work, as long as it remains ' personal ', acquires no impetus. It builds up no objective tradition to act as a fly wheel, for there is no machinery to distribute and sustain its force. It precludes organization. Each parish is ' run as a one-man show '. The church is described as ' Mr. So-and-So's Church'. The curates become mere hangers on, handy-men doing odd jobs—' too old at forty '. *Work limited to one man.*

This limits the area of work to the parish. Care for detail is important, of course, and the parish should be the training-ground for the diocese. But parish work, as things are now, tends to be made up entirely of petty matters such as in secular business are delegated to young women or entrusted to agents and clerks. The outlook becomes parochial, unthought out and narrow. The work, too, is inevitably confined to a few persons in the parish since it is impossible, as we saw, for an individual to touch directly more than a limited number, and, as we saw, beyond the power of one man to ' know ' more than, say, fifty people in any intimate sense of the word. *To the parish*

this Committee's request for information, in spite of a prefatory letter from their bishop, is suggestive of much.' Again we find that in the same Diocese, ' In replies to inquiries sent out by the Diocesan Board of Finance only 405 out of 600 parishes made returns.'

Kept down to the level of one man.

In addition, all such personal work is not only limited but also kept down to the level of the individual, since no stream can rise higher than its source. His peculiar personality permeates everything. Through the preaching and the services, in the music and the ceremonial, his accent can be heard. At best it is only one man's power that is working, and no man is perfect all round. The work even of a strong despot is singularly insecure, as Laud failed to realize.[1] Where a man is weak, vulgar, or uneducated, the result is disastrous. The false ideal condemns the mass of parish churches and their life to a low dead level of mediocrity. Moreover, every man—even the best—becomes exhausted or old in time. The type of work hastens such exhaustion, and there is no removal or recovery.

Alienating more than it attracts.

The power of ' personal ' or individual influence is limited always. It is not only limited to a few in number but its hold is precarious. See how it failed in the case of George Tyrrell in his early days, or in that of Robert Benson,[2] or, to take an example from what is confessedly fiction, in that of the young hero of Mr. Mackenzie's *Sinister Street*. Besides it repels with equal force when men are antipathetic, and many people—the majority perhaps—dislike it intensely. For one man who is pleased at being fussed about with, two are probably driven away. Even where natural and good in adolescence, it is a continually decreasing power as the subject passes on to manhood, and often there is a violent reaction. Boys who were ' got hold of ' in youth generally

[1] W. E. Collins, *Lectures on Archbishop Laud*, Archbishop Laud Commemoration (Southey & Co., Printers), 1895, p. 49 : ' He failed simply because a kingdom is larger than a college. In the comparatively narrow circle of the one, a strong personality is agile to impress itself upon the whole body and stereotype itself by the sheer force of its individuality. But in the larger unity, the will of the whole body has freer play, and the single personality cannot diffuse itself universally. . . . The Archbishop grappled manfully with the vast mass of public business, keeping all he could in his own hands because he could not trust others to do thoroughly what had to be done.'

[2] *Confessions of a Convert*.

resent it bitterly afterwards. The peculiar animosity of
those who break with a party or community—there is no
need to quote examples—is attributable to the feeling that
they were unduly influenced and their independence not
respected. The bitterness that runs through the pages of
the Reminiscences of Mark Pattison, that ' escaped nun '
of the Tractarian Movement, exaggerated, is typical. As
Dr. Jowett said of Newman's following at Littlemore, ' It
wasn't fair on those young men '.[1]

The foundation of all such work is rotten at the best, for
it substitutes material and social for spiritual influence.
When we have visited and shaken hands for a year we have
at most only achieved a social success. We have still before
us the whole task of turning social into religious influences,
and sometimes we find that all that we have done is to turn
a religious into a social force. ' If I go away at Whitsuntide,
I once heard a vicar say, ' the communicants suffer.' In
many cases this personal intercourse may be very undesir-
able. It is doubtful whether it is wise, even socially, for
a man to disregard all social conventions, and to go calling
on women of quite a different class, in whose ordinary life
the social call plays no part. It is not clear that the pride
with which a woman tells her neighbours how the Vicar
called on her, is altogether a good thing. Sometimes there
are elements which, though the clergy are happily generally
unconscious of them, are distinctly ' unpleasant '. In
certain cases there is danger of blackmail on the part of the
unscrupulous ; in all such there is grave danger of misunder-
standing among husbands away at work. Of course, where
the visit arises naturally out of the carrying on of some
work, and the visitor pays, not a social, but a business visit,
such danger practically does not exist, but even so the underlying assumption that the social visit of a parson is in itself

*Substitu-
ting social
interests for
religious.*

[1] For a justification of Newman's use of personal influence see Wilfred
Ward's *Last Lectures* (Longmans), 1918, Lecture V, ' Personality in
Apologetics,' pp. 102–23.

of such great spiritual import seems, when we come to think of it, to be tinctured with a certain flavour of conceit.

Often
dangerous.
The undesirableness of this kind of personal influence is recognized in the school world. 'Machinery, machinery, machinery,' wrote Edward Thring, who certainly knew what he was talking about, 'should be the motto of every good school. As little as possible ought to be left to personal merit in the teacher, or chance ; as much as possible ought to rest on the system and appliances on every side checking vice and fostering good, quietly and unostentatiously, under the commonest guidance and in the most average circumstances.[1] A certain percentage of crime must result from inadequate machinery and neglect.'

'A more subtle danger (than that of merely imposing himself on his pupils) surrounds this problem of personal influence. . . . When a teacher has so trained her class that they " will do anything for her "—it is often a sign that her work is mischievous.'[2] In the Army, authority that is purely personal is bad for discipline. 'Though it is a fine thing when men trust their leader and follow him anywhere, it is still finer when they will stand by any leader whether they know him or not, and this last is the fruit of perfect discipline.'[3] 'There is nothing perhaps more characteristic of

[1] *Life and Letters of Edward Thring*, G. R. Parkin (Macmillan), 2nd ed., ch. iv, p. 92.   See also p. 64 : ' It may dazzle men more to watch a great man's success under adverse circumstances, but it benefits society more to have a good strong system set on foot which any average honest man can work.'

[2] J. J. Findlay, *Principles of Class Teaching* ; Macmillan's Manuals for Teachers, 1911, pp. 390–1.   See also J. Adams.

[3] The comment of ' A Student in Arms ' in *The Spectator* for January 1, 1916, on the following story of a N.C.O. who gave an order which a man refused to execute. He should have been put under arrest, but the N.C.O. ' looked at the man contemptuously and went and did the job himself. He had not been at the job two minutes before the boy came and joined him.' ' The N.C.O.', he continues, ' certainly gained the respect and confidence of his men, and there is no possession better worth having from the point of view of the individual ; but his authority was purely personal, and, on the whole, bad for discipline. He was to realize it

a superficial period of civilization, of a lazy superficial
unthinking attitude on the part of man than the foolish un-
critical idolatry of what has been called personality in others.
It means, as a rule, the hypnotizing and gradual enslavement
of the will.'[1] Enthusiasm for a cause is generally noble.
' Schwärmerei' about a person is always a little ridiculous.

When we look round at the task before us in the world,
at the problems to be solved, at the work to be done, at the
truth to be taught, and the issues at stake ; when we think
of the masses in our towns, or of the ever extending lines of
solitary farms in our Colonies ; when we contemplate the
growing flood of ignorance and vice, and the swelling of the
sea of troubles that threatens to overwhelm us ; and then
when we consider our reliance on ' personal work ' we cannot
but think of Mrs. Partington and her attempt to drive back

a little later. An officer who was in charge of a big working party called
for two volunteers to accompany a corporal in stalking a German sniper.
Not a man volunteered. After some minutes, during which the officer
appealed and rated in vain, a boy came to the N.C.O. and asked " who
is the corporal that is going ? " The N.C.O. replied that he did not know.
" Oh," said the boy, with obvious disappointment, " if it had been you
I would have volunteered." For the corporal it was at once his reward
and his condemnation.'

J. Adams, *The Evolution of Educational Theory* (Macmillan), 1912,
p. 36 : ' In many cases it is the educator's duty to efface himself. The
educator of vigorous personality and strong motor temperament is very
apt to think that he is doing excellent work when he is letting off his
energies in strenuous teaching, while as a matter of fact he is repressing
the activities of the young people who ought to be doing their share, and
are not permitted. Even intellectual work may be conducted so as to
weaken where it should strengthen. Consider what underlies the following public eulogy of a distinguished teacher :

" His students had such implicit confidence in his knowledge and
such reverence for his opinion that after leaving him they no longer
cared to think for themselves. They were satisfied by the conclusions
reached by a mind so superior to their own, possessing a grasp and
insight which they realized was so far in advance of anything they
could ever hope to attain."

Meant as a panegyric this is really an indictment of the teacher in
question. It is a proclamation of disastrous professional failure.'

[1] A. L. Lilley, *Adventus Regni* (Francis Griffiths), 1907, p. 120.

the Atlantic with a mop. Our method, like hers, may be excellent for a slop or a puddle—and of course they need to be wiped up—but for anything more we need one other and better.[1]

III

The real nature of personal work.

To understand the nature of personal work that really deserves the name, we may turn to Our Lord's parables. Many of them are based on the analogy of spiritual life with agriculture and farming. Just as a change has come over all processes of work on the land, so a change is needed in work for the harvest of souls and the flock of the Church.

A place for individual work.

Not that the need of individual work has been done away with. It still holds its place among the rank and file of the labourers. It is useful, often necessary, for the farmer to go through the apprenticeship of toil, since it will make him practical and will keep him in touch with reality. Important work, too, is being done by the Veterinary Surgeon, who treats sick animals one by one. Stock breeding, and the production of new varieties of plants by cross-fertilization, must remain skilled work done by the individual expert. So much might be done, no doubt, were the clergy more accessible to the people. It would be a good thing if more would offer themselves in the public parks to answer questions on the difficulties of religion. If they attended at

[1] Sydney Smith, *Works* (Oxford), 1840, vol. iv, p. 393. *Speech at Taunton*, October 12, 1831 : ' I do not mean to be disrespectful, but the attempt of the Lords to stop the progress of reform reminds me very forcibly of the great storm of Sidmouth, and of the conduct of the excellent Mrs. Partington on that occasion. In the winter of 1824, there set in a great flood upon that town—the tide rose to an incredible height— the waves rushed in upon the houses, and everything was threatened with destruction. In the midst of the sublime and terrible storm, Dame Partington, who lived upon the beach, was seen at the door of her house with mop and pattens, trundling her mop, squeezing out the sea water, and vigorously pushing away the Atlantic Ocean. The Atlantic was roused. Mrs. P.'s spirit was up ; but I need not tell you the contest was unequal. She was excellent at a slop or a puddle, but she should not have meddled with a tempest.'

certain hours in the church as in an office, people would feel
as free to come to them as to any other officials at their posts.
So it was the accessibility of Ambrose that played a distinct
part in the conversion of Augustine, for, we read, ' the door
was open to all and no one was announced.' [1]

But even so, for the most part, the initiative must come
from the laity.   Otherwise the parson's individual efforts,
vague and undirected, will result in a terrible waste of time.
Even such work done in response to a demand is at best
limited and unsatisfactory.   Ambrose when Augustine
visited him was obviously busy.   ' I could not ask him what
I wanted, as I wanted,' he writes, ' because the shoals of
busy people, to whose infirmities he ministered came between
me and his ears and lips.'   ' Often when we attended, after
sitting some time without speaking we went away again.' [2]
As he lets us see in his *Confessions*, it was the bishop's readiness to help that attracted him, rather than anything he
could find to say in the brief audiences that were given.
He was far more affected by the influence of his work exercised unconsciously, by stepping into the cathedral without
being interfered with by a verger, and listening to him
there.[3]   Later on Augustine himself, as his biographer
Possidius tells us, used to spend whole days interviewing
people, but his great work was quite other.   His service to
the humanity of his day was rendered by his action in
Councils ; to posterity by his writings.

So if in special cases individual personal work is indispensable, it is always more valuable when it is part of a
larger undertaking, and in general it would be fair to say that,
with the evolution of society, men are less and less affected
or helped by direct personal influence (at any rate in proportion to other influences) just as its power is strongest over the
young, and continually weakens as they pass to maturity.   Spiritual
life a
For spiritual life is a growth, not a manufacture.   This is   growth.

---

[1] Possidius, *Vita Sancti Augustini*, ch. ix.
[2] *Confessions*, Bk. VI, ch. iii.   [3] Ibid., Bk. V, ch. xiii.

involved in the pastoral imagery of the New Testament.
Paul plants and Apollos waters, but God gives the increase.
The work of helping our fellow man in his relations to God
(if we take this as our definition of Pastoral Theology) consists largely in weeding, in preparing, and in irrigating, the
soil. The Church of the Apostles spread far less by direct
missionary effort and much more by natural growth than
we are apt to think.

The art of
letting
people
alone.

We want sadly, then, to learn the art of letting people
alone, of opening locked churches, of offering the spectacle
of big congregations in big churches, where people can enter
and be caught up in the spiritual atmosphere, without feeling
that they will be pounced upon by vergers, shaken hands
with by the clergy, and asked if they may be called upon,
or noticed and gossiped about by the congregation.[1] The
ideal secretary is he who sets things going so that they grow
and develop without his interference, while he is set free for
fresh work and new opportunities.   If he sinks his personality in his work it extends just so much farther. ' I venture
to think,' wrote Mr. Shorthouse, ' that just as far as " the
priest " loses himself, so to speak, in the sense of prayer, or
of sacrament, or of service, i. e. thinks of the sense and not
of himself, he will find acceptance and result from his
congregation.'[2]

Working
with
natural
forces.

If religious life is a growth there is all the more need that
we should work with the great forces, natural and spiritual,
that guide and sway the destinies of men. This is now
realized in education which began by elaborating its teaching
matter, then learned to think of the training of the teacher,
and now has finally realized that it is the child that really
matters.   We need a similar study of applied psychology
in Pastoral Work to find out what are the needs and interests

[1] T. Fowler, Progressive Morality (Macmillan), 1895, p. 182 : ' The
lesson of letting other people alone is one which men are slow to learn,
though there are few who, in their own case, do not resent any attack on
their liberty of judgement or action.'

[2] Life of J. H. Shorthouse (Macmillan), 1905, vol. i, p. 300.

of men. For new customs cannot be invented ; they must spring up spontaneously from seeds, and need time to grow. Where new practices are self conscious and stamped with individual characteristics, it is the old and impersonal rites and ceremonies that seem to us ' the real thing ' and are accepted by all as interpreting their inner needs. This is the strength of a Catholic Christianity such as ours, that its features have obtained because they are broad based upon universal human instincts.

Religious life is not merely a growth ; it is a complicated one. It has shared in the change which has come about in society, and is therefore little helped, even where it can be touched, by individual effort. This is obvious if we consider, for instance, the enormous development of hotel life, not only in London but in seaside and other watering-places. The whole lives of a certain class are spent in boarding-houses of various sorts, where they are lived quite apart from the more normal life of the neighbourhood. To wait on these persons there is a whole army of servants, male and female, and for the religious life of neither class does the Church, with her present methods, reckon, any more than she does with the large body of night-workers, of pressmen, of actors, of those employed on Sunday, of officials in institutions, of commerical travellers, or of men living in bachelor chambers. Men read and hear all sorts of opinions. They get their ideas from numbers of journals of all shades of opinion, from illustrated papers, from open air speakers. Individuals themselves, too, are much less simple. The educated have to form their convictions from a continually increasing array of data, and the uneducated, if unable to make any coherent synthesis of their various impressions are none the less influenced by them in varying degrees, since every influence has its force.

Personal work, therefore, can only be expected to tell along the already existing lines of the social structure in which men live. The elaboration of relationships between

[margin note: A complicated growth.]

[margin note: Natural relationships.]

man and man, while they bar the way to the individual intruder, form channels for influence of a strong personality. This is seen in schools where the character of the head master tells all through the forms, in the army where the men unconsciously take their tone from their officers, in a business house where one department will be palpably different from another because the head in one is a man of good manners and of consideration for others. Men holding official positions can take a real interest in the lives of those to whom they have official responsibilities. It is much appreciated if the head of a firm takes an interest in the house sports, if the Dons go to the college football matches, if the officer sees to the comfort of his men before thinking of his own. This is something quite different from making yourself cheap in order to ' break down prejudice ', or doing unnatural things in order to show a professional sympathy.

It is just the ideas that are in the air that it is impossible for men to resist. The belief that it is an adequate description of the Church to say that she is Protestant, or that she ' teaches that you will go to hell if you do not (say that you) believe ', or that Christianity is bound up with the doctrine of verbal inspiration, have hardly been touched by fifty years of preaching and teaching in Sunday Schools. For such ideas are of long standing and cannot be altered in a day. Others are often the result of sustained effort ; the spirit that prompted the splendid work of the Y.M.C.A. in providing recreation rooms for soldiers was no new one, and the Church could not extemporize any thing to compare with it. The fact that the enormous labour of compiling English Theological Dictionaries has mainly been under Presbyterian and Nonconformist influence will not be counteracted by sermons ' arranged on Monday '. If ideas arise from many causes they will not be greatly modified by any single action. The mass of them influence men in many ways, and therefore, to meet them, and to Christianize them, we need sustained policy in all departments of church work.

Therefore in all things we have need of policy. We must seek out the causes and springs of evils and counteract them at their sources. These are sometimes clear but many. If we consider, for instance, the prevalence of betting, its extent and organization, how sporting papers live for it, how ordinary evening papers rely on it for their circulation, so that news-boys automatically cry ' winner ' whether there is any racing news or not ; when we think of the armies of lads who are being sacrificed to it by being dragged down to street selling ; of the horde of parasites in the shape of bookmakers who live on it and become centres of corruption in normal society [1]; of the squandered fortunes and of the wasted wages ; of the sufferings of wives and children ; of the burden of pauperism falling on the struggling and honest who have to support those who have wasted their opportunities ; of the dishonesty and crime that accompanies it ; of the corruption of sport and the degradation of the intelligence that is due to it ; it will be realized that, rooted as it is in so many kinds of soil, it will not be eradicated by merely preaching sermons about it.[2]

So with such a question as the evil of prostitution with all its wide ramifications of organized wickedness; obviously it cannot be preached about. There are needed all sorts of methods equally organized and systematic ; methods of

The need of policy.

Checking evil at its sources.

[1] In the *Daily Mail* of November 11, 1911, we read : ' It seems that the Flushing bookmakers pay about £8,000 a year in postage and £5,000 a year for telegrams. They employ 160 clerks and contribute £1,000 a year in taxation.'

[2] Matthew Arnold, *Culture and Anarchy* (Smith Elder), 1869, p. 30 : ' Another newspaper, representing one of the religious organizations of this country was, a short time ago, giving an account of the crowd at Epsom on the Derby Day, and of all the vice and hideousness which was to be seen in that crowd ; and then the writer turned suddenly round on Professor Huxley and asked how he proposed to cure all this vice and hideousness without religion. I confess I felt disposed to ask the asker this question : And how do you propose to cure it with such a religion as yours ? '

instruction of youth, of co-operation with the police, of watching of places of amusement, or of open spaces, of newspapers and shops, methods of preventive and rescue work. All this must necessarily be on a scale larger than the parish and must be the work of specialists and experts.

Or consider the question of the disrespect in which the clergy are held ; a disrespect which reacts on religion itself where the ' personal ' element is so much over-emphasized. Positive dislike may not be altogether a bad sign. When men are doing good work they are certain to be abused by those who feel that they have become a reproof to their thoughts. But the symptoms of a mild disrespect can be seen everywhere—on the stage, in music halls, in novels, in *Punch*, in little stories told in private conversation. It arises from numerous causes, from little tricks of voice and manner, from inadequate capacity to perform official duties, from the self-consciousness that makes men awkward when insecure in their position, from lack of observation that makes them make mistakes in dress or suffers them to smoke in just those streets where it strikes the laity as bad form, from failure to realize when they are not qualified to give an opinion on subjects outside their province, from tactlessness in introducing religious questions at inopportune times because they have never thought out the question of the conditions of religious propaganda, or in failing to bring them in at the right time and so giving the impression that they ' are ashamed of their job '. We need a steady policy that will go behind all these causes, that will reform our training for Orders, and will start men on the lines of sufficiency in their calling, surely, the only way to make it respected as other callings are respected. These are all questions of movements rather than of men.

Causes often other than appear. But in all such cases it will soon be realized that there is more behind than appears at first sight. A direct attack, if not found useless, will soon be seen not to be enough. The evil of betting depends ultimately on human nature and on

the view of work and wages that generally prevail. In proportion as men take pleasure in thorough work will they
feel that reward is only due for things done. In proportion
as to get money without doing anything for it, and to live
without adding to the world's wealth, is considered dis-
graceful, betting will disappear. The underlying evil of
prostitution is the general survival of the pagan conception
of woman and her place in the world. This is widespread in
quarters other than those that are obviously vicious. In
the press, on the stage, in fashion plates and in ' ladies'
pages ' of daily and weekly papers, in sentimental songs, on
picture postcards, in the labour world, in second-rate
girls' schools, the false idea is still powerful. The battle for
purity is being fought wherever men are working for a new
attitude in education, in the shop, or in the home.

Missionaries find that the chief obstacle to their work is
the behaviour of the nominally Christian white man. The
problems of foreign missions, in other words, lie largely at
home. Even in direct mission work it is the theology of the
mother country that is taught. It is in England that the
majority of books must be written, from England that the
general policy must be directed, and in English colleges that
the pioneers at any rate must be trained. No final result
can be got by the strict supervision of music halls and
cinema films. To attack indecency is only to advertise it.
The only thing that can successfully purify our places of
amusement is the decency and taste of the masses. As soon
as the majority showed that they preferred a clean perform-
ance the mass of performances became clean. When the
war gave a stimulus to lubricity there was a distinct decline
in the type of entertainment offered. But the masses are
trained in decency by religion in fields far distant from the
places where the issue is decided ; they form their taste at
home, in the school and in church. It is doubtful if Jeremy
Collier's attack on the Restoration Drama would have
succeeded had there not been at the time a real and strong

church revival. So, again, modernism in novels can only be insufficiently met by reviews ; a profounder theology and the training of the critical sense generally among churchmen will be far more effective in making it harmless. Atheistic propaganda must no doubt be answered, but its chief causes are probably to be found in a false theory of inspiration taught by ill-read Sunday School teachers, in boredom caused by long unintelligible services in church during youth, and in irritation fostered by antagonizing methods of controversy. If these were cured its main-springs would probably be gone. Such questions as these are questions of ideas even more than of particular action.

Causes often obscure.

Sometimes the symptoms are difficult to judge of, and the causes equally obscure. The relation of white men to subject races presents a problem which can only be worked out with infinite patience and forbearance. To ignore the difference is almost as fatal as to adopt the ' d——d nigger attitude ', but between the two there are infinite possi-bilities. The relations of poverty and wealth to-day are obviously wrong. We feel that there is clearly something out of joint when we see a lady in a motor with three grown men entirely occupied in waiting upon her ; still more strongly do we feel it when we see one of them occupied in taking her little dog for a walk. That she should employ a number of people solely in cleaning unnecessary things cannot be right. The evil is not met by schemes of confis-cation by the State, yet the problem how to create such a sentiment as will make such things impossible is not easy even to outline. Or again, as in Coleridge's day so in ours, 'there is no hope of converting the Jews in the way and with the spirit unhappily adopted by our Church; and indeed by all other modern churches.'[1] Argument is not likely to convince by itself. Religious bribery is certain to fail. It would seem as though the first step must be the acceptance of the Christian standard of life and then the conscious

[1] *Table Talk*, April 14, 1830.

adoption of Christian ethics, then might follow the assimilation of Christian customs, and, as they come to inquire what these are based on, the acceptance of Christian theology as the explanation of their value, while the last step will be the practice of Christian worship and the admission into the Christian covenant by baptism. These and other such questions present problems which must be studied before we can even begin to set ourselves to mental fight in the realm of ideas, but in all cases, whether in the study, in ideas, or in definite external action, the Church must be working in many different centres, with steady, sustained, far-seeing, and consistent policy.

IV

If this be true it will alter the whole nature of our work. We shall find out that the important things are quite other than those which have been engaging our main energies. We shall come to see that what really matters is doing good work with a clear aim and leaving it in faith to tell by its own force. We shall turn our attention to big things, to matters of Church reform, to finance that will provide pensions for the clergy when past their work, or scholarships and colleges to give adequate training before they begin it. We shall organize strong centres of teaching and preaching other than parochial. We shall pursue a definite line in building fine churches worthy of the purpose to which they are to be put. We shall look out to discover the sources of men's thought, for the springs of movements, for the groundwork of character. Our attention will be directed to our schools and to the whole work of education. We can begin anywhere. Good work in any part will affect the whole.

The remedy of good work.

But we shall have to reverse our whole idea of what work means. We shall have to learn that it is done mainly by the head and little by the muscles ; that it is carried on in committees, at the desk, in silence, by study. It will

Reversing popular ideals.

demand greater self discipline, for where any one (except a cripple) can rush about a parish or diocese, it needs far greater energy to think things out, more concentration of purpose to sustain continuous action, and more patience to guide others as a good general, and to get the work out of other people. But it will bring us back again to religion as the real thing that matters in human life, and by internal discipline and belief in intellectual and spiritual things, will make seem reasonable to us the power of prayer.

CHAPTER V

THE POINT OF ATTACK

' We grant, indeed, that the good which higher governors do is not so immediate and near unto every of us, as many times the meaner labours of others under them, and this doth make it to be less esteemed. But we must note, that it is in this case as in a ship ; he that sitteth at the stern is quiet, he moveth not, he seemeth in a manner to do little or nothing in comparison of them that sweat about other toil, yet that which he doeth is in value and force more than all the labours of the rest put together.'— HOOKER, *Ecclesiastical Polity*, Bk. VII, ch. xviii, § 4.

THE transition from management to government as the chief factor in the life of society has involved a necessity for policy in all things, and has made possible a science and practice of politics. In this science two rival theories of government have from the beginning disputed the field, and they are still disputing it. On the one side aristocracy, in its various forms of hereditary monarchy, of tyranny, of oligarchy, even of much so-called democracy like that of Athens which was based on slavery, or like that of Imperial Rome, which under the forms inherited from the day of the Republic, gave the real power to the Emperor or to the Army—and on the other side democracy, whether working through a constitutional monarchy, or through elected and changing representative bodies—each have their advocates and apostles. *Two rival political theories.*

The upholders of aristocracy argue for their theory by an appeal to the history of institutions and of political thought. They point out that in the slave-based states of Greece Plato and Aristotle were on their side, and that even the democracy of Athens, limited as it was, distinguished itself by putting Socrates to death. They remind us that tyrants brought wealth and prosperity to the cities that they governed, that under them the arts flourished, that France *Aristocracy.*

saw her era of typical greatness under Louis XIV. They turn from the past to the present and urge the facts of the contrast between conservative Ober-Ammergau and progressive Manchester, or point to the general vulgarization of society in comparison with the often quoted ' good old times '. They instance the habits of the self-made man, and lament that districts are ' going down '. Turning from facts to theory they urge the *a priori* folly of allowing yourself to be guided by the ideals of the lowest, and point to Russia in confirmation of their assertion.

Democracy.   On the other hand, the democrats argue that Christ taught the poor and pronounced a blessing on their estate, that the preaching of the gospel to the poor has been the great force in the world since He came. They remind us how the barbarous northern tribes received as conquerors the laws and civilization of the conquered without their corruption and effeteness, and so created our vigorous modern world. Turning to special instances they declare that great art can only be built up on a broad popular basis, that music rests on folk-song,[1] that poetry depends on allusiveness in common speech and on clear and sonorous articulation in everyday life, that the great factor in forming the thoughts of the nation is the popular daily press. To improve these, they argue, is the only way of raising the people as a whole. They remind us of the failure of the Jesuits in South America who ruled their converts for their good *de haut en bas*. We do not need that they should remind us of the failure of Prussia in everything except what has been spontaneous and has arisen from the heart of the German peoples. But in the cross and counter fire of argument the real criterion is generally lost sight of. The question is not one primarily of policy but of character.

[1] It has been suggested that English music has failed to rise to excellence because it has been exotic and eclectic, that it is on the lines of music-hall melodies, at present vulgar beyond description, though with a vigour and sense of rhythm that never seems to fail, that a really national school can be evolved.

The issue is, in fact, not between Conservative and Liberal, capital and labour, employer and employed, aristocrat and democrat, but between Christian and Pagan. What is needed for the betterment of the world as a whole is, on the part of the rich, self-sacrifice, because all wealth, whether of money or of ability, is a trust from God ; that they should follow the example of Christ, who though rich became poor, rather than that of the kings of the Gentiles who try to earn the name of benefactor by exercising authority—and on the part of ' the poor ', readiness to learn, willingness to reverence and trust those endowed with higher qualities than are they themselves, to be at once without suspicion and yet discontented with low ideals and the present limitations of their lives ; that is, that they too should follow the example of our Saviour, believing that the meek inherit the earth rather than the grasping and aggressive. In each case all depends on duty being put before rights, on giving being preferred to getting.

For there are two methods of doing good. You may start from below and work upward. If this way is chosen you deal with masses. You make a broad popular appeal. Your instruments are the daily press and the public speech. You reckon with ideas in the air. You turn to children and to the schools rather than to grown-ups, to anticipate the time to come. For in this way you reach the masses, who are gradually rising to rule, by direct attack.

Two methods of doing good.

Working from below up.

Or you may work from above down. In this case you will seek to deal with men in small numbers, even one by one, because you single out the men who count, and they are few. There are never many men at the top, but it is they who lead, who influence, who create, who originate the ideas and customs that are taken up and adopted by the masses below.

Working from above down.

So Christ drew His disciples out of the people it is true, but, having done this, He seems to have preached little to the multitude. His life work was mainly to train a few to be pillars and groundwork of a Catholic Church.[1] St. Paul, again, it is true, initiated a mass movement, but even this was largely because he was a great man, chosen for his qualities to preach to the Gentiles, and, ultimately, in the course of the world's history, his chief influence has been that which has worked on us through the thirteen letters which he wrote.

I

Faults in Church policy.

Both methods, that of working from below up and that of working from above down, have their advantages, and both have their dangers. In modern Church policy the faults of both seem to be combined. We have concentrated our chief efforts on ' the poor ', thus adopting the less effective plan ; and we have done this in the spirit of patronage, which is the peculiar danger of the method of working from above down.

The method of direct attack.

It is part of the popular idea of ' church work ' that it is ' among the poor '. ' There can't be much to do in that parish,' people say, ' as there are so few poor.' We send our best men to East London because we are conscious of our failure there, but do not consider the causes of that failure, or whether it may not even be aggravated by our sending them. For our method of immediate attack is, to say the least, the direct contrary to that of nearly all other activities. In politics, a school that wishes to gain adherents subsidizes and issues a weekly magazine continuously for years. In learning we concentrate our efforts in universities, and from them go out journalists, teachers, and leaders of all sorts. Women have made great efforts to secure the right to study and be examined at Oxford and Cambridge, because on that depended the character of the girls' schools of the whole country. It may be right that the Church should adopt a method directly opposite, and we

[1] Cp. H. Latham, *Pastor Pastorum* (Cambridge : Deighton, Bell & Co.), 1890, pp. 225-7.

often boast that ' the Church alone seeks out the poor ', but we have no right to assume that these others do not care for them. Tested by results we have failed most lamentably, as was shown eighteen years ago by Mr. Charles Booth,[1] and as we rediscovered when the calling up of men to the army revealed the almost complete alienation of the masses from the Church to which they nominally belonged.

Certainly this method of direct attack is the hardest and most costly, for we begin with just the men from whom we are furthest removed, and with whom we have fewest points of contact. ' Work amongst the poor ' is often chosen by young men ' because it is the hardest ', without distinguishing between work that is hard because it is difficult and should therefore be undertaken by the experienced, and that which is hard because it is heavy, and therefore the sort that they can best do. In reality, work in poor districts is the lightest because there is so little that can be done. The clergy are never really in touch with the people approached except at a few superficial points. No doubt a vast amount of unnecessary and ineffectual labour is gone through, but very little of it is in contact with the spiritual life and experience of those whom it is meant to help. It is largely irrelevant, and cannot be compared with the real work that is going on in a parish where there is a large practising Christian congregation. This false relationship, too, leads to false methods. We are over-intellectual, appealing by words to men's reason just where the educated and uneducated have least in common. We preach, we talk, we give tracts, we circulate parish magazines written in our own literary style, we set those whom we describe as ' the poor ' to sing hymns written in language they never use, we argue, we explain, and we are surprised that it has so little effect. Our habits, again, are different. We visit people who themselves never pay calls. We ask people to tea parties in

The hardest

[1] In his *Life and Labour of the People in London*, 3rd Series (Macmillan), 1902, *Religious Influences*.

schoolrooms whose idea of social enjoyment is the bean-feast, or we invite them to meals in our houses where they are intensely uncomfortable from the difference of our social customs. Worse than that, we adopt a patronizing attitude. We talk about ' what they think '. We assume that ' Tommy can't stand much religion ', as if a private soldier were an essentially different being from ourselves. We adopt an amused attitude towards the working-classes in repeating little stories of what they say and do. These, perfectly justified in the pages of *Punch*, which they probably never see, we print in parish magazines. In these pages we mimic their mispronunciation of words by incorrect spelling, and actually distribute them in the houses of those whom we are laughing at.[1] We shake hands continually with them, and doff our hats emphatically on meeting them in the streets, because we imagine that ' they like it ', without realizing the false attitude involved in doing to them what we should never do to our social equals. These are some of the blunders that seem inevitably to accompany the method of direct attack.

and most costly.

This is not to deny a certain measure of success to such efforts. Where good men work conscientiously, even by blundering methods, some advance is sure to be made. But the method of direct attack exacts a heavy toll on our resources, and many of its results are disastrous. Among these may be reckoned contentment with a low standard of work. We remain occupied in elementary teaching and satisfied with elementary ideas. Renan said somewhere that the result of a nation having only an elementary education can be seen in the general vulgarity of a people ; so the effect of our almost exclusive attention to the lower classes can be seen in the general degradation of ecclesiastical taste. The standard of our hymns, of our music, of our preaching, of our art, of our architecture, is kept down to the popular level. The whole is mean and uninspiring. We are

[1] I believe that *The Sign* (Mowbray) never offends in this way.

dominated by inferior ideals. This, in turn, tells in the type of worker that we employ. The tone of public worship is largely set by uneducated and immature choir-boys. Our church arrangements are to a great extent controlled by the notions of vergers. Especially serious is the growing number of men of inferior education who are seeking Holy Orders. By Ordination these rise socially and become out of touch with, and disliked by, men of the class from which they have come, while, owing to the inadequate training that we give them, and to what Mr. Barnabas Oley styled ' praeproperous ordinations '[1], they remain hampered by their old limitations. And the unfortunate thing is that this is the price we are paying for the measure of success with which our efforts have been directed so exclusively to poor parishes.

Meanwhile, among ' the rich ' the case is going by default. Some are being definitely alienated. It has often been pointed out that if ' men of science ' are out of touch with the Church much more so are the artists. Others, including the great mass of the cultured and educated, are being ignored and neglected. Their ignorance in simple matters of Christian belief and practice is reflected in our weekly reviews and monthly magazines. Yet these men are proving the real power in the country. The politicians, the writers, the teachers, the officers, the artists, are the men that count, but they, and with them the masses whom they influence, are left, as far as the Church is concerned, for the most part, religiously untouched and uninterpreted.

The ' rich ' neglected.

Therefore we want a complete reversal of plan. The call to repentance is one to a *metanoia* or change of mind. We want to get rid of the old tactics of patronage, of merely

[1] Preface to George Herbert's *A Priest to the Temple* in *The Clergyman's Instructor*, 4th ed., 1827 (Oxford), p. 10 : ' You have rightly pitched upon two sluices that let into the Church men not rightly qualified : (1) promiscuous admission into the universities, (2) indiscriminate or praeproperous ordinations ; which latter is often but a consequent of the former '.

trying to work from below upwards, and we want to concentrate our forces on the best, to work from above down,
as the surest way of influencing both the men that matter
and the masses whom they lead.

II

The case
for the
democratic
method.

This is not to say that the method of working from below
up is to be entirely neglected. We may even continue our
present work if the spirit can be changed. Anything that
does any good may well be kept on, and those who still think
this is the best way may continue their efforts provided they
do not deny the possibility of any other.

The up-
ward trend
of society.

For there is much to be said for the democratic method.
Let us make out its case. As a matter of fact it falls in with
certain great movements of society. We see symptoms of
these in the growth of our suburbs. Complaints are often
heard from older residents that districts are ' going down '.
In reality they are going up. Mere fields are being turned
into gardens. Men and women, producers of wealth, are
taking the place of the wealth of fruit and flowers which
they create. Houses for them to live in, often mean enough
and ugly, are taking the places of barns and sheds, pic-
turesque perhaps but serving lower purposes than the
upbringing of children and the storing of the fruits of
domestic life. The people, too, who are swarming out
from the still meaner city streets, are going up ; in dress, in
appearance, in bearing, in manners, in habits of life, in
refinement, in interests, they have reached a higher level
than that of their parents and their youth. They are
bringing up with them working-class ideals, expanding
them and developing them. There are whole areas where
there is practically nothing of an older and higher civilization to correct their tastes and to guide their lives. Young,
vigorous, hopeful as they are, it is small wonder that unpleasant features among them grow strong. They bring with

them the slang, the accents, the outlook on life, that are drawn from working-class conditions. Our self-made men find their pleasure in motor-cars, in noise. Their tastes are catered for in music-halls and pantomimes. They are in possession of our watering places. They enforce and strengthen the general trend towards materialism if only because they are but recently emancipated from conditions in which material cares pressed on them only too instantly. What is true of districts is true also of nations. What so often (and without other or good reason) offends us in American habits and ways is that they are frequently developments of what at home still remains characteristic of the lower middle classes. In ecclesiastical life the predominance of nonconforming Protestantism in the religious life of our colonies is largely due to the fact that Dissent has been in the past most vigorous among the peasants and, more recently, among the dwellers in the suburbs.

Further, it may be conceded that the existence of the lowest class is a continual drag on those just above, both socially and morally. Black areas, to adopt Mr. Charles Booth's name for the worst slum districts, draw others down. An increase of pauperism causes a burden which always falls heaviest on the poorest, and continually tempts those just above the line of independence down into dependence. Crime encourages crime and vice is contagious as diseases are contagious and spread from uncleansed centres of dirt and ill drainage. The work of rescue has to be done, just as we must have special schools for the mentally deficient, homes for orphans, reformatories for the criminal, and hospitals for the sick. But these are neither so great in extent, nor so profitable in themselves, as are the prevention of fall, the rearing of children healthy in body and mind, family life, and religious upbringing. The latter are the chief, and are part of the normal life of all. The abnormal is the exception. *The drag of the lowest class.*

Again, it is a fact that work which is broad-based on an *The appeal to numbers.*

appeal to the masses has a great advantage in extent, and that to the Christian every soul counts. Its area increases in geometrical proportion as we descend the social scale. This was recognized in the War, when the problem of thrift among the masses was seen to be so serious. Cinemas have flourished because they have relied on the ' nimble sixpence '. The influence of journalism depended on the appearance of the penny daily, and that in turn is largely giving way to the halfpenny press and the Sunday paper. Advertisement pays because it appeals to the million. All this is not ignored by other agencies. Those who worked for the extension of the franchise to women did not neglect the open air platform of the Parks. The Workers Educational Association is doing a great work among artisans. There is a great value in the Settlements which prevent the untold harm of districts developing without any representative of a higher standard of education and culture in their midst.

A measure of success. And we may grant that the efforts of the Church do meet with a real measure of success. All honour to those who are endeavouring to stop evils at their sources. It is a real glory to the Church if she seeks out those whom others neglect, and it is not only in India that Pariahs have been raised so as to outstrip the privileged Brahmin in education, character, and morals.[1]

But, for all that, the rise of men of lower classes is due far more to their copying those just above them than to the efforts to raise them made by those far above. This is seen most obviously in dress, but it may be heard in language also. Working people are catching the habit of ejaculating ' sorry ' as an apology, of calling things ' rotten '[2], of saying ' sir ' to one another when not acquainted. It is marked in

[1] Cp. G. E. Phillips, *The Outcastes' Hope*, 5th ed. (Church Missionary Society), 1918, pp. 83 ff.

[2] The following conversation was recently overheard in a Tube lift :
' A ye gettin on, Bill ? '
' Rotten.'
' Swell's wy o' talking, en it ? '

manners, but the gradual filtering down of upper-class
standards in morals and thought is seen for good in the
steady spread of sobriety downwards, and for evil in the
growth of luxury due to imitation of the extravagant.[1]
With Hooker we can ' easily declare how all things which
are of God He hath by wonderful art and wisdom sodered
as it were together with the glue of mutual assistance,
appointing to the lowest to receive from the nearest to
themselves what the influence of the highest yieldeth '.[2]

III

So the soundest policy is to go for the best. Even the
virtue of the opposite method of working from below
upwards depends on the elimination of bad ideas by their
finding, as they rise, no atmosphere in which to flourish, so
that they wither and die, and on the preservation of the
good by their finding that environment in which they alone
can come to their own. Many men are lost to the Church
because, though trained in churchmanship as boys, they
find no fuller Christian interpretation of life as they pass on
to maturity, no ampler presentation of Christian practice
as they pass from country to town, or from slum to suburb.
Just as taxation always filters down, and in the long run
falls on the poorest, so learning, culture, ideas, and with

Going for
the best.

[1] ' Ostentation,' writes Mr. Withers, ' perhaps owing to the efforts of
a Press that gives much of its space to telling the suburbs what the
leaders of society are doing, has spread itself all the way down the
various strata of the middle class, which used to distinguish the comforts
of life from its fripperies with some success.' *Poverty and Waste* (Smith
Elder), 1914, p. 68.

[2] *Ecclesiastical Polity*, Bk. V, ch. lxxvi, § 9. Cp. also Bk. VII, ch. xviii,
§ 7 : 'The mean man's actions, be they good or evil, they reach not far,
they are not greatly inquired into, except perhaps by such as dwell at the
next door : whereas men of more ample dignity are as cities on the tops
of hills, their lives are viewed afar off ; so that the more there are that
observe aloof what they do, the greater glory by their well-doing they
purchase, both unto God whom they serve, and to the state wherein
they live.'

them religion, filter down. When Cobden declared that his main interest was in the conditions of the lower class, Matthew Arnold wrote, ' But I am convinced that nothing can be done effectively to raise this class except through the agency of a transformed middle class. For, till the middle class is transformed, the aristocratic class, which will do nothing effectively, will rule '.[1] Left in isolation by itself the lowest class can be helped but little.

The importance of great men.

So, without neglecting our present work among the poor and crippled, we ought to be directing our main energies to the biggest men, to the men who count. Augustine in his *Confessions* analysed the causes why we rejoice more over the conversion of famous men—' because they are known to many, they influence many toward salvation, and lead the way which many will follow '. It is not that the rich are accepted before the poor, or the noble before the lowly, but that, as in the case of St. Paul, ' the enemy is more utterly beaten in one in whom he has more hold, and through whom he has hold of more '.[2] As the tallest trees

[1] *Letters of Matthew Arnold* (Macmillan), 1895, vol. i, p. 224.

[2] *Confessions*, Bk. VIII, ch. iv ' Si minus noti sunt populis, minus de illis gaudent etiam qui noverunt eos. Quando enim cum multis gaudetur, et in singulis uberius est gaudium, quia fervefaciunt se, et inflammantur ex alterutro. Deinde, quod multis noti, multis sunt auctoritati ad salutem, et multis praeeunt secuturis. Ideoque multum de illis et qui eos praecesserunt laetantur, quia non de solis laetantur. Absit enim ut in tabernaculo tuo prae pauperibus accipiantur personae divitum, aut prae ignobilibus nobiles : quando potius infirma mundi elegisti ut confunderes fortia ; et ignobilia huius mundi elegisti et contemptibilia et ea quae non sunt tanquam sint ut ea quae sunt evacuares.—Plus enim hostis vincitur in eo quem plus tenet, de quo plures tenet. Plus autem superbos tenet nomine nobilitatis, et de his plures nomine auctoritatis.'

(' If they are less known to the people, even those who know them rejoice for them less. For, when joy is shared by many, the joy of each is richer, because they warm one another, catch fire from one another. Again, because they are known to many, they influence many towards salvation, and lead the way which many will follow. Therefore, even they who took the way before them rejoice over them greatly, because they do not rejoice over them alone. For far be it from us, that in thy tabernacle the persons of the rich should be accepted before the poor, or the

are most moved by the wind, so the examples of the greatest
men are most conspicuous.[1] Dante was only shown the
spirits ' whom fame hath note of ' :

> For the mind
> Of him who hears, is loth to acquiesce
> And fix its faith unless the instance brought
> Be palpable, and proof apparent urge.[2]

So in literature there are thousands of second rate phrases,
while a few classic expressions stand out as well known by
quotation, because they exactly sum up in perfect form

noble before the lowly, seeing that thou hast chosen the weak things of the
world to confound the strong; and the base things of this world and things
despised hast thou chosen, and things that are not, that thou mightest
bring to nought things that are. . . . For the enemy is more utterly beaten in
one of whom he has more hold and through whom he has hold of more.
And he has the more hold of the proud by means of their rank, and
through them he has hold of more by means of their influence.'—Tr.
C. Bigg, Methuen's *Library of Devotion.*)

Cp. Browning, *Luria*, Act 5, near the end :

> A people is but the attempt of many
> To rise to the completer life of one.
> And those who live as models for the mass
> Are singly more of value than they all.

[1] Horace, *Odes*, Bk. II, 10 :

> Saepius ventis agitatur ingens
> Pinus, et celsae graviore casu
> Decidunt turres, feriuntque summos
> Fulgura montes.

(When high in air the pine ascends
To every ruder blast it bends.
The palace falls with heavier weight
When tumbling from its airy height.
And when from heaven the lightning flies,
It blasts the hills that proudest rise.
                Tr. Philip Francis, 1747.)

[2] *Paradiso*, Cant. xvii. l. 133 :

> Questo tuo grido farà come il vento,
>   Che le più alte cime più percuote :
>   E ciò non fa d'onor poco argomento.
> Però ti son mostrate in queste ruote,
>   Nel monte e nella valle dolorosa,
>   Pur l'anime che son di fama nòte :
> Chè l'animo di quel ch'ode non posa,
> Nè ferma fide per esempio ch' haia
>   La sua radice incognita e nascosa,
>   Nè per altro argomento che non paia.

some piece of human experience put in words by a master, and are worth whole volumes of the others. We feel powerless as individuals to combat thoughts that are, as we say, ' in the air ', and these are largely due to the work of great men. The present day misapprehension of the nature of dogma is largely due to the work of Harnack. The influence of Wordsworth, of Coleridge, can be traced in almost any movement of the nineteenth century.

Of the up-
per classes.
It is not only through the most important individuals that we should try to work ; we should concentrate our best efforts on the upper classes. Dr. Arnold worked through his sixth form, knowing that so he would reach the smallest boys in the school.[1] St. Patrick converted Ireland through her tribal chiefs.[2] ' Class D ', rather than the submerged, thinks Mr. Rowntree, ' the better class working man, is the one to which social reformers should direct their efforts.' [3] Christianity, as a matter of fact, first spread

---

[1] A. P. Stanley, *The Life and Correspondence of Thomas Arnold, D.D.* (Ward, Lock & Co.'s *Minerva Library*), 3rd ed., ch. iii, p. 70 : ' My own school experience has taught me the monstrous evil of a state of low principle prevailing amongst those who set the tone to the rest. I can neither theoretically nor practically defend our public school system, unless you assume that the upper class shall be capable of being in a manner μεσῖται between the masters and the mass of the boys, that is, shall be capable of receiving and transmitting to the rest, through their example and influence, right principles of conduct, instead of those extremely low ones which are natural to a society of boys left wholly to form their own standard of right and wrong.'

P. 79 : ' The chief source of his intellectual as of his moral influence over the school was through the sixth form. To the rest of the boys he appeared almost exclusively as a master, to them he appeared almost exclusively as an instructor.'

[2] Cp. J. B. Bury, *The Life of St. Patrick* (Macmillan), 1905, p. 74.

[3] *Poverty*, B. Seebohm Rowntree (Macmillan), 3rd ed., 1902, p. 79 : ' It is important to remember that, taken as a whole, Class ' D ' is that section of our population upon which the social and industrial development of England largely depends, and is the one which will always exercise the most important influence in bringing about the elevation of those in the poorer classes.

' It is clear, therefore, that effort cannot be too largely directed towards

among the educated.[1] The great advance of the Church was in the second century, when having conquered the family she conquered the schools.[2]

So we ought to be sending our best men, not to the East, but to the West End. We should concentrate our strength at the universities rather than in the parish. We should make our point of attack the men in the suburbs rather than ' the poor '. We should strengthen the Christian and preach to the well-disposed first, and so let our message spread and permeate society.[3]

Again, we should work from strong centres. That this is best is amply proved from history, by the example of Alexandria, Lerins, Rome, Lindisfarne, Port-Royal, or Oxford. For we are at our best in congenial society with ' religious intimates congenial, hearers thoughtful, and the realization in Class ' D ' of a higher ideal as regards personal character education, and home life. The fact that members of this class are not handicapped by poverty should greatly facilitate the attainment of this end.'

Working from strong centres.

[1] W. M. Ramsay, *Cities and Bishopricks of Phrygia* (Oxford), 1897, vol. i, pt. ii, p. 517 : ' The educated section of the population was, on the whole, that which first turned to Christianity ; the unthinking mob of the great Greek cities and the uneducated rustic population were the last to be affected by it.' Cp. F. Cabrol, *Dictionnaire d'Archéologie chrétienne,* art. *Aristocratiques (Classes),* Tome I, 2me Partie, pp. 2845–85.

[2] Cp. B. F. Westcott, *Essays in the History of Religious Thought in the West* (Macmillan), 1891, p. 195, *Origen and the Beginnings of Christian Philosophy* : ' The Church and the Empire started from the same point and advanced side by side. They met in the market and the house ; they met in the discussions of the Schools ; they met in the institutions of political government ; and in each place the Church was triumphant. In this way Christianity asserted once for all its sovereign power among men by the victory of common life, by the victory of thought, by the victory of civil organization. . . . The period during which this second conflict of the Faith was waged was, roughly speaking, from the middle of the second to the middle of the third century.'

[3] I have lost the reference for the following : ' He advised a young clergyman to begin by addressing the best informed and best disposed in his congregation ; they would help to reform the ignorant and reprobate. If you had to kindle a promiscuous pile of wood, where would you apply your light, to the green sticks or to the dry ? '

friends sincere '.[1] The action and interaction of soul and soul brings out what is best in us. The isolated worker is dragged down to the level of the society round him, or is shut up in himself. A man cannot do his best work alone, and becomes spiritually atrophied if he abides by himself. This is a fact which is reckoned with in work by committees and councils, in universities and schools, and in all collegiate and coenobitic life. For the sake of the masses we must create strong centres. ' It is plain,' writes Professor Harnack, ' that at the end of the fourth and at the beginning of the fifth century, there was a spiritual awakening everywhere in connexion with the growing adoption of monasticism by persons of education.' [2]

This will mean, at first at any rate, that we must be content with smaller numbers. It is right to be *austère* as St. Francois de Sales found *La Mère Angèlique*, and to be fishers of fewer but bigger men.[3] We want to work by what has been called the intensive rather than the extensive method.[4] The strength of early Oxford Tractarianism

[1] Bp. Andrewes' *Devotions*, The Fifth Day, *Praise*.

[2] A. Harnack, *Bible Reading in the Early Church*. Eng. Tr., by J. R. Wilkinson (Williams and Norgate), Crown Theological Library, 1912, p. 129.

[3] C. A. Sainte-Beuve, *Port-Royal* (Paris), 1860, vol. i, p. 219 : ' Quand il s'enquit près d'elle de la manière de vivre tant à Port-Royal qu'à Maubuisson, il la trouva austère et lui dit : " Ma fille, ne vaudroit-il pas mieux ne pas prendre de si gros poissons, et d'en prendre davantage ? " '
(' When he asked her about their way of life both at Port-Royal and at Maubuisson he thought her (or it) too strict, and said, " My daughter, would it not be better not to catch such large fish and to catch more of them ? " ')

[4] W. Hobhouse, *The Church and the World*, Bampton Lectures, 1910 (Macmillan, 1910), Lect. VIII, p. 321 : ' It is now widely recognized that if a mission is to produce permanent results, it must pursue a policy of concentration rather than of diffusion. There will always be some diffused work going on round the centre, but the centre itself is the important thing.'
P. 301 : ' Have we any settled policy as to whether the methods of the Church should be primarily extensive or intensive, whether (that is) quantity should be preferred to quality or quality to quantity ? '

lay in the fact that it was primarily an educational movement, based on a belief in sound learning, occupied with certain features of university reform, and directed towards the teachers of the masses rather than to the masses themselves.[1]

The intensive method demands a high standard of work. We must hold to the belief that good work tells. It involves more walking by faith, for we shall see less immediate result of our efforts. It will specially demand a better training of the clergy, to educate men with eyes to see and brains to devise, alert, ready to suggest, with character to act on their convictions and to carry their undertakings through. Such will avoid offending those who know, if they have at least the power of recognizing expert knowledge when they come across it. They will not alienate experienced social workers by their crude amateur philanthropy. They will not drive away the musical by choosing bad hymns. As the spire of St. Pierre at Caen became the prototype of many another beautiful steeple in Normandy, so the example of a high standard of work in one parish will be felt all round.[2]

Of a high standard of work.

Finally we shall turn our attention to big things. It is big things that especially appeal to men. If we want congregations not entirely feminine we must build big churches, even if we have to close small mission rooms. We must turn to broad issues, and away from exclusive preoccupa-

Of big things.

[1] Mark Pattison, *Essays*, ed. H. Nettleship (Oxford), 1889, vol. ii, p. 269: ' The High Church leaders had other recommendations above their learning. But at the first rise of the Tractarian School above the horizon in 1833, and before its other features were obliterated in one desperate effort of assimilation to Ultramontanism, it was instinctively felt to be a revival of the spirit of learned research. Hugh Rose, Newman, R. H. Froude, and Keble, were first awakened by the study of primitive antiquity in its original remains. The new leaders were recognized by all the orthodox party as descendants in the direct line from " our great divines ".' See also J. H. Newman, *Idea of a University*, Discourse vii, § 3.

[2] F. Bond, *English Church Architecture* (Oxford), 1913, vol. ii, p. 950.

tion with details. We must insist on the things that matter, and let go unimportant and small affairs. It has been suggested that Athanasius left the people out of account, that his appeal was always to the theologian and professionally religious. This was not so, but he saw that the greater included the less, and his action was justified by success.[1] The Church knew very well what she was about when in her councils she insisted on a right belief in the person of Christ, for on the theology of the learned depended

Working through these on the masses. in the long run the faith of the people. But all our concentrating on big men, on the upper classes, on work from strong centres, by a high standard, and on big things must be done with a consciousness of the needs of the masses, and because we believe that it is the surest way of helping them. It is for their sakes that we must consecrate ourselves. We need not drop our present methods of direct attack (so long as they are not too costly), but we want to add to them, to build up the whole structure of these other methods. They are the more effective because they lead instead of driving the people, because they seek them by methods of co-operation rather than of aggression, because they work with the natural aspirations of men to things greater and higher, because their influence, though unseen, is continual and all pervading, where the personal method of direct approach is limited and exhausts itself in its effort.

IV

An aristocracy of religion. Therefore, since the spiritual factor in life is the one that it is the peculiar mission of the Church to uphold, we need to create an aristocracy of religion. Our churches, our theological colleges, our community houses must be homes of prayer. Just as the universities were founded to uphold a high standard of learning, so should these be centres of knowledge of the Eternal Wisdom. Just as society exists

---

[1] A. E. Burn, *An Introduction to the Creeds* (Methuen), 1899, p. 97.

to be a school of fine manners and to give free play to the graces of human intercourse, so these should be centres of worship in the beauty of holiness and provide scope for disciplined intercourse with God. We want areas where the Christian moral standard is accepted without question, in which life is deliberately based upon it and lived by it without let, where, without apology, it is judged by Christian canons, and without the necessity of striving or crying the Christian outlook on the world is assumed. This will not, or should not, make men priggish any more than human culture need make them affected. It will not, or should not, make them out of touch with practical life any more than a university education need make men merely academic. We want to secure free course for a great stream of natural un-self-conscious spiritual life, spreading from such sources in our midst ; a spiritual life that shall avoid the weakness that comes from individualism in religion, and at the same time escape the eclecticism that besets monastic piety if cut off from contact with the great onward flow of common human life that is lived in the workshop and in the home.

But this aristocracy must continually bear about within itself the thought of others and for their sakes hallow itself. *For the sake of others.* The Church as catholic must be democratic as well as aristocratic, and must include, interpret, and serve, all. Her catholicity is perpetually threatened by the existence within her of class customs. There are, of course, differences among men, and different men have different needs, but we must see to it that the belief in the virtue of the best does not harden into a system of caste, or service degenerate into mere benefaction. Free intercourse is necessary between classes if only to keep clear the way for the inflowing of that which one needs and another has got. Especially must this influence be allowed free course between those who stand nearest one another in station, ability, or interests.

Great
things ap-
peal to all.

The greatest things are always the simplest and so suit all. We want to work for clear, broad, strong issues in life and in worship, issues which shall be intelligible to the simple and shall provide a foundation for the complex to be built on. In our forms of service we want a simple structure that will bear elaboration ; in our preaching clear outlines that will not be obscured to the unlearned by the richest embroidery of rhetoric and illustration ; in our cathedrals and churches the simple plan that can admit of fullest richness of detail ; in our teaching clear principles of right and wrong that run through all the complicated problems of daily life. For human nature is at bottom one and all men love the highest when they see it.

CHAPTER VI

THE FIELD OF BATTLE

Καλὸν γὰρ τὸ ἆθλον καὶ ἡ ἐλπὶς μεγάλη (Noble is the prize and great the hope), PLATO, *Phaedo* 114.

WE have traced some of the influences of industrialism in creating the society of which we are part, and have tried to discover some of the changes in church work that are imperative if the Church is to do her work in the new fields of battle on which the issues of right and wrong are to be decided. We have seen some of the results in life domestic, urban, personal, and political. But behind all these external worlds there is the intellectual and moral world within. _{Industrialism and materialism.}

To-day's world of thought has not just leaped out fully-armed from the brain of Hephaestus. It is the result of a long process in many minds, passed on from generation to generation. We have travelled far from the ' Ages of Faith ' as they are called, those times of a smaller and simpler world when there was less to know and do, so that industrial and social interests were not, and could not well be, dissociated from those religious and ecclesiastical. _{The ' Ages of Faith '.}

The way to change was opened up by the Reformation, with its social upheaval and its disintegration of thought, and by the advancement of learning that had begun with the Renaissance and made specialization in study seem so much more natural. The first great step forward was made in the purely abstract science of mathematics. The interest, confined in the seventeenth century almost entirely to the science itself, spread out into life as a whole in the eighteenth, the ' Age of Reason ', when fundamental theological and philosophical problems were being thought out, and so prepared the way for the idea-ridden French Revolution _{Mathematics and Rationalism.}

and the German Aufklärung, the two parent streams of modern English Rationalism.

Development of machinery But already in the eighteenth century the world was seeing a practical application of mathematical science in the development of machinery. This reacted on thought and instinctively predisposed men to a mechanical and Deistic view of the universe.[1] Side by side with it came a great increase in the number of mechanics, and this increase was from the social strata to the members of which philosophical religion appealed but little, while, from political and social causes, they had largely lost touch with any living and organized religious practice. The Evangelical and Wesleyan movement came too late to prevent the masses of the people from being predominantly irreligious.

Increase of wealth. The nineteenth century reaped the result of industrial mechanism in an enormous increase of production and in the consequent wealth. At first the possession of the masters, it was soon shared by the middle classes, and presently the masses had their part in the growth of comfort and in the rising standard of life. Invention followed invention, and process succeeded process. Material things loomed large, especially among the growing middle classes. Recruited as they were from the most vigorous and practical of the irreligious masses, the appeal of practical materialism was to them almost irresistible. Moreover, it was backed

[1] ' Some men have so used their heads to mathematical figures that, giving a preference to the methods of that science, they introduce lines and diagrams into their study of divinity or political inquiries, as if nothing could be known without them ; and others, accustomed to retired speculations, run natural philosophy into metaphysical notions and the abstract generalities of logic ; and how often may one meet with religion and morality treated of in terms of the laboratory, and thought to be improved by the methods and notions of chymistry ! ' J. Locke (1632–1704), *Conduct of the Human Understanding*, Section 24, *Partiality*. For the tendency in the eighteenth century to interpret everything in terms of Mathematics see the references under Mathematical Analogy in the Index to Leslie Stephen's *History of English Thought in the Eighteenth Century* (Smith Elder), 1876, to which may be added the following in vol. ii, pp. 96, 191, 211, 230, 269, 270, 343, 351.

up by the whole movement for political freedom which, as it happened, was largely associated with Positivism as a theory of life and Utilitarianism as a ground of morals.

Meanwhile intellectual activity had been concentrated on the physical sciences, and not unnaturally, considering its enormous advance and bewildering discoveries in all directions. So much was this the case that they usurped the name of Science in popular speech, and men still normally speak of ' Science ' when they mean ' Natural Science '. This has taken away, even from many of the more educated, any real sense of the need of the higher sciences of Sociology, Ethics, Psychology, Philosophy, and Theology. It has made widespread a general deprecation of dogma, that is of the results of theological science, and of the use of reason in the hi er spheres of human knowledge, while it has created an unbounded confidence in the powers of the intellect, trained in material and practical schools, to decide all questions unaided by any other human faculty.

Physical Science.

For one hundred and fifty years these forces have been operating on the great masses who have surrendered themselves, for the most part, to the influence of externals. In Germany we have seen the result with awful clearness in the great final appeal to force which utilized all the science, skill, and wealth, that had been the inheritance of the last century and a half. It commandeered philosophy and art with its theory of Kultur. It bent education to its will. Where it could it exploited Christianity, and where it found that impossible it has openly repudiated its sanctions, declaring that necessity knows no law, and that might is right.

Modern Society.

Peace will hardly touch the intellectual and social forces that have been working so long. Victory over one form of their manifestation has not put an end to their influence. The question before us still is whether our future civilization is to be Christian, whether, as Dr. Creighton asked, the fruits of Christianity which have so far survived can be preserved without Christianity itself.[1] This is the great problem of the future, for Christianity is the saving factor in all departments of life.

I

Aimlessness of life

It is the saving factor in the externals of society. The first thing that strikes us on a superficial view of life around us is its general purposelessness. The war, no doubt, showed that there were many more than perhaps we thought who could show a definite sustained purpose, that there were many who were only waiting for their opportunity. In a way it has even strengthened the sense of purpose in men and women. But this largely depended on the stimulus of urgent need, and even to that many failed to respond. There are masses of men and women still who have no resources but futile amusements, who have no artistic or literary tastes, who rush about the country in motor-cars and periodically overeat and overdrink themselves.[2]

and letters.

Even to take refuge in literature and art brings us little farther. Our present-day writing is marked by a depressing lack of inspiration. A broad stream of tiresome novels

[1] *Life and Letters of Mandell Creighton* (Longmans), 1906, vol. ii, p. 191. *Letter to Mr. Charles Roundell* : ' Most people . . . want to work back to Christian principles by minimizing them. This is called " undenominational Christianity ", i.e. as much fruit and as little root as possible. A popular audience will always cheer a reference to " true religion stripped of the bonds of theology ", i.e. the results of the Christian conscience without the faith which formed it. Of course we have now reached the actual question of the present day. This underlies the education question, this animates the Deceased Wife's Sister and all the rest. It is the great question of the future.'

[2] M. W. Keatinge, *Studies in Education* (Oxford), 1916, p. 103 : ' Few things are more striking in adult life than the number of persons who have no means of artistic expression or appreciation at all ; who are driven for relaxation to futile pursuits such as card playing, and who, as their higher feelings atrophy, become, in success, fonder of their food and drink, and possessed of a morbid craving for rapid motion ; or in failure, gloomy, listless, and irritable.'

issues from the press among which the few that have some
purpose stand out as conspicuous exceptions. The rest
amuse perhaps, are clean and harmless, are well written,
but have no point. The same is true of much of our poetry
of to-day. It peters out like a path in a wood that leads
nowhither, if it does not deliberately exercise a cult of
ugliness. This may be in part a mere criticism of conser-
vatism which says that :

> Few and fewer do they grow
> Who know, or ever cared to know
> The great things greatly said and sung
> In this heroic English tongue

and declare that all that is popular in literature to-day is
' the loose-lipped lingo of the street ' or ' the beaded and
bespangled style ' in

> An empty and a dreary strife,
> Vulgar in letters as in life.[1]

No doubt we all grow old and fail in sympathy with the
new. But that is not the whole tale. There is something
lacking in most of our modern literature which it is at first
difficult to detect. The feeling as we read is evasive and
hard to analyse, but the result is perceptible to the sensitive
reader just as a defective education or a deficient sense
of humour is felt at once in certain estimable and clever
persons. The lack is due, I contend, to the absence of
Christianity in the lives of the authors. The most vigorous
writing without it is only true to life as Macbeth saw it,
' a tale full of sound and fury, signifying nothing '.[2]

There is a strong and widespread feeling that we need   Music.
an English school of music. There are diligent workers in
the field. By choir competitions and by choral societies
enthusiasts are doing much to spread a love of song. But
here again we are met by the same futility. Our composers
have gone to the German words of Heine for their songs.

[1] Sir William Watson, *Retrogression and other Poems* (John Lane), 1917.
[2] Act V, sc. v.

Englishmen write music for the Latin Mass. Cantata writers, having exhausted the Bible, scour poetry books for words to set for Festival Performances. Others, realizing the mistake of such academic exercises, are collecting and diffusing folk-songs. They realize that national music must be broad-based on national singing, and they are met with the over-whelming fact of the modern music-hall with its vitality, its apparently inexhaustible vigour, and, withal, its utter vulgarity. The only rival that can challenge it is the Church. Religion alone provides a general opportunity for the life of common song, as is abundantly seen in Wales where hymnody is a living art.[1] Religion alone can provide an adequate motive for good popular music both vocal and instrumental. As a matter of fact our numberless (if indif-ferent) church choirs represent a great undertaking ; were secular choral societies to exist in half the number we should never stop talking about them. Mr. Falconer's seven sister domestics at the Folly, who played and sang to their master every evening in dresses of white and purple, would be impossible in real life ; [2] there is nothing unseemly or unnatural in a household, family and servants, uniting to sing hymns or anthems at evening prayers in a chapel day by day.

Painting.

Browning has drawn the contrast between limited and perfect, and therefore unprogressive, Greek art, and Chris-tian art, whose reach exceeds its grasp but has time in store, and his lessons from the fifteenth century are as valid for the twentieth as he saw them to be for the nineteenth.[3] His three examples of failure represent permanent types.[4] Pro-gress in architecture, the greatest of the arts, has depended on a similar contrast. The triumph of Christianity in the

Architec-
ture.

[1] Cp. T. R. Glover, *The Christian Tradition and its Verification.* The Angus Lectures (Methuen), 1912, p. 180 : ' It has to be remembered, too, that the hymn-book is in the main a Christian product. Cleanthes wrote a sort of hymn to Zeus or fate ; but nobody sang it.'

[2] T. L. Peacock, *Gryll Grange*, ch. v.   [3] *Old Pictures in Florence.*

[4] *Fra Filippo Lippi, Andrea del Sarto,* and *Pictor Ignotus.*

fourth century effected a revolution in that it concentrated artistic effort on the Christian church as the Greeks had before made its centre the temple, but with this difference, that its aim was ' to inspire a congregation gathered within it and not to attract the gaze of worshippers outside '.[1]

So, for the great mass of the people, their church is the one place where their feet are set in a large room, and architecture is the greatest of the arts. Apart from purely domestic art, that of the church, with its stained glass, its painting, and decoration, its music, its oratory, its literature, its ordered motion of worshippers, its ' long-drawn aisles and fretted vaults ', is the only art available for them, and religion is the only force strong enough to create such centres of beauty in our villages and in the poorer quarters of our towns. All great art is public art.[2] The fault of the soul that built her ' lordly pleasure-house ' was that she built it for herself alone. The Palace was not to be pulled down as the Puritans would have destroyed it. The guilt-purged soul looked forward to her return ' with others there ',[3] and so may it be in our day.

Ultimately these questions of the externals of life are questions of the education that we give to the individuals that are to make up society. Of education two rival theories are in the field ; that which holds that a child is sent to school to learn useful facts and advertises the opportunities of ' salary-raising education ', and, set against this, that which regards schooling as directed to the balanced development of the whole man, fitting him to enter into life in this world and the next, and, in entering, to understand

Education.

[1] W. Lowrie, *Christian Art and Archaeology* (Macmillan), 1901, p. 89.
[2] Cp. B. F. Westcott, *Religious Thought in the West* (Macmillan), 1891, p. 340, *The Relation of Christianity to Art* : ' When Greek Art was greatest it was consecrated to public use ; and one chief danger of modern society is lest the growth of private wealth should lead to the diversion of the highest artistic power from the common service, and at the same time leave the appropriate labours of domestic art discouraged.'
[3] Tennyson, *The Palace of Art.*

and interpret rightly all he sees around him. To enable a man by education to have life more abundantly, the one effective factor is religion. It alone can adequately inspire the great mass of teachers. It has unique opportunities of supplying the matter by which body and mind are trained, and it works from within, where, too often, mere instruction influences solely from without.[1]

II

Ideals of life.

The question of religious education is important because the teaching of home and school determines the aim of life. The ideals which guide men's actions, the subjects which exercise their thoughts, the standards by which they judge, the inner life, that is, is of vastly greater moment than the externals of art and culture.

The cult of health.

Prominent among the preoccupations of men to-day is the cult of health. It has its good side. No one would wish to go back to the old days when invalids like Elizabeth Barrett were kept lying in stuffy and darkened rooms. The wonderful discoveries of medical science, the perfecting of surgical and nursing skill, have saved countless lives. Many a man is now working in full vigour with his appendix removed who would have been lost to the world had he lived a generation ago. More important than all perhaps, a better knowledge of infant life, diffused by the work of health societies and Schools for Mothers, is resulting in happy childhood and adult vigour. But this close attention to health is reacting on character. We are said to be becoming more sensitive to pain. The English devotion to sport is causing uneasiness to those who value the things of the mind. More serious still is the fact that the cult of health is becoming a new religion to many and is usurping the place of the old. In Christian Science we find the assump-

---

[1] I have treated this subject more fully in my *Introduction to the Study of Pastoral Theology* (Oxford), 1912. Bk. III, ch. ii, Pastoral Theology and Education. See also below, p 165.

tion that the pursuit of good health is the essence and end of religion accepted without question by large numbers of indifferently-educated people. Vice often shelters itself under the cover of Eugenic propaganda. Now Christianity has never made light of suffering or minimized the importance of the health that comes from self-control, but its central doctrine of the cross has emphatically declared that physical soundness stands second to spiritual health, and that pain of the body is often the price of the salvation of the soul. The Passion of Christ as redeeming the world is set forth by the Church in diametric opposition to the merely Eugenic creed.

Christianity, besides, works in clear antagonism to the commonplaceness of the masses. The only ideal of life that numbers of men seem to have, it is said, is that of ' having good time '.[1] Even if we take into account the Englishman's unwillingness to declare his deepest motives and his inability to analyse them and express them if he would, this judgement would seem to be true of a vast proportion of the people, and opens up a sufficiently dreary outlook. Men are often better in fact than in their theories, as has been shown in their abundant kindliness in the trenches and in the hospitals, in their unfailing readiness to think others worse off than themselves. Many, too, after a purposeless and idle youth find salvation in marriage, in living for and loving wife and children. But how much is lost from lack of a clear ideal of life ! How narrow in outlook is the man with no religious practice ! He has no beyond, and oppresses us like a stuffy room where the window, which is never opened, has no more distant view than that which at Todgers's ' commanded the opposite archway '. And the pathetic thing is that men think that they are broadminded in not going to church and in seeking to ' have a good time '.

'Having a good time.'

See a painfully interesting article, *The State of Religion. Some Evidence from the New Armies*, in the *Church Times*, February 25, 1916.

Greater command of the means of life does not mend matters. Our self-made men have grown out of a society that has learned the value of money but has had no clear idea of the responsibility that attaches to its possession, so that having it has simply led to greater vulgarity. When we think of the enormous waste of culture among those who have the means to do things, how England might be filled with noble cathedrals and beautiful works of art with the better spending of what is wasted daily, when we realize how much actual poverty is caused by this waste, how all the setting people to do useless things by those who can order it by their wealth takes them away from doing useful things that would make the lives of their fellow-workers more easy and would give them the opportunities that they so sorely need [1]—when we realize all this we see the utter contrast of the ideal of simplicity in life, of the blessedness of those who are poor in spirit even though they possess wealth, of the conception of riches as a trust from God and not as a possession, of life as consisting in what a man is and not in the abundance of things he owns, of property as that which is spiritual and within and therefore inalienable, which can be shared with others without ' exclusion of participants in good '.[2]

[1] I know no better exposition of this theme than that in Mr. Hartley Withers's *Poverty and Waste* (Smith Elder), 1914.

[2] Dante, *Purgatorio*, Canto XIV, l. 86 :

> O gente umana, perchè poni il cuore
> Là 'v' è mestier di consorto divieto ?

Canto XV, l. 49 :

> Perchè s'appuntano i vostri desiri
> Dove per compagnia parte si scema,
> Invidia muove il mantaco ai sospiri.

Canto XV, l. 61 :

> Com' esser puote che un ben distributo
> I più posseditor faccia più ricchi
> Di sè, che se da pochi è posseduto ?

> Quello infinito ed ineffabil bene

> Tanto si dà, quanto truova d'ardore ;

Among the ' have nots ' we find the same stress laid on money. They are, to invert the beatitude, 'rich in spirit'. But fuller means of life do not constitute the chief needs of the artisan and labouring classes of to-day, so much as a fuller conception as to wherein life consists. The general acquiescence in a lower standard of manners, such as, for instance, leads them to remain seated in a tram while women are standing,[1] or to keep their hats on indoors, shows itself most conspicuously in the general indifference to the disgrace of drunkenness that forms the staple subject of ' comic ' songs, which is growing slightly less, and the

> E quanta gente più lassù s'intende,
> Piu v'è da bene amare, e più vi s'ama,
> E come specchio l'uno all' altro rende.

(O man, why place thy heart where there doth need
Exclusion of participants in good ?

Because ye point your wishes at a mark
Where, by communion of possessors, part
Is lessened, envy bloweth up the sighs of men.

How can it chance, that good distributed,
The many, that possess it, makes more rich
Than if 't were shared by few ?)

               (The highest good,
     Unlimited, ineffable . . .
     Giving as much of ardour as it finds

.   .   .   .   .   .
     So that, the more aspirants to that bliss
     Are multiplied, more good is there to love
     And more is loved ; as mirrors that reflect
     Each unto other propagated light.)

Cp. Augustine, *De Civitate Dei*, Bk. XV, cap. v ' Nullo enim modo fit minor accedente seu permanente consorte possessio bonitatis, immo possessio bonitas, quam tanto latius, quanto concordius individua sociorum possidet caritas.' ' For the possession of goodness is by no means diminished by being shared with a partner either permanently or temporarily assumed ; on the contrary it is increased in proportion to the concord and charity of each of those that share it.'—Tr. Marcus Dods (T. T. Clark), 1897.

De Doctrina Christiana, Lib. I, cap. i ' Omnis enim res quae dando non deficit, dum habetur, et non datur, non habetur, quomodo habenda est.' (For any thing which grows no less in giving, and is had and not given, is not had with a true having.)

[1] The common belief that ' working men are much more polite ' in this particular will not survive half a dozen journeys in the Tube before 8 a.m.

indescribably filthy language which is accepted as natural in the army or the workshop, and has grown notably worse in the last generation. The latter may be excused on the ground that it arises among uneducated people from their lack of powers of expression, and that the word used has lost all its meaning, but that makes it no less serious in its result. It makes them tongue-tied in the presence of their betters, for they are afraid to speak without offending, and it has a continually besmirching effect on their minds even if they do not think of the real meaning of what they say. Moreover a very slight effort could overcome it, as is proved by the fact that foul language was rarely heard in Y.M.C.A. huts, and in hospitals where the sister was present men would bear excruciating pains without an indecent word. An elementary sense of religion diffused among the masses would stop it at once to the enormous uplift of the nation. The power of self-control is there abundantly in men who can cheer others when themselves dying.[1] It only needs the adequate motive. Such men could do anything with the grace of God accepted to rule their whole life.

Economic waste.

The economic waste of bad work is enormous. The army of inspectors found necessary to see that men do not idle when paid by the hour, or scamp their task when paid by the piece, that men do not travel without tickets, or make false income-tax returns, represents sheer loss of time and service to the community. The cost of malingering under the Insurance Act, of fraud in the drawers of old-age pensions, even with all this inspection, adds seriously to the burden of the people. The necessity for almost the whole

[1] Extract from a private letter. 'Then again the restraint of the wounded men is wonderful. In the ambulances they swear and curse. I have been with men and held their hands while the Sister is unavoidably giving them gip. They sometimes shriek, but do not swear. You can imagine how painful it is to have . . . It was a man with both legs off. . . . After I left the orderly told me that in spite of his pain he had been cheering the patients the other side of the ward. . . . I wrote to his mother. . . . However bad a man is he generally believes that some one else is worse . . . and his sympathy for others is intense.'

organization of the law courts is a continuous drag on prosperity. Our police courts, our prisons, and, to a far too great extent, our hospitals and madhouses, represent the price that is paid for vice.

On the other hand, the fact that we have general confidence in people's honesty, that, for instance, we can assume that change will be correctly given, and the goods ordered sent, makes the whole fabric of commerce possible. A very slight increase in the number of absolutely trustworthy people would stand for an increase in millions in national wealth ; a small additional defect would spell commercial ruin.

The diffusion of economic knowledge can do much. If trade union leaders can be got to see clearly that you cannot increase wealth by restriction of output and idleness, nor better conditions of whole classes by limiting the number of skilled workers, a great deal will have been done. But the economic question is primarily one of religion. Its business is to stop ' the old envenomed quarrel between employer and employed ', to foil the appeal to passion and to the distrust of others by showing that it is based on untruth, to cut away the ground from malingering and ' ca'ing canny ' by showing up its dishonesty and making men feel that dishonest things must not be done.

In all social work evil conditions can be directly traced to moral causes. This is irresistibly impressed on you as you take part in any thorough and organized work that goes deeply enough into the matter. While surroundings tell, the heart of the matter lies in character.[1] This is true not only in the causing of social disease but in its cure. It all depends on how far you can count on a response to your efforts to help, or how far you can rely on a supply of workers with a sense of responsibility. A small change,

Social work.

---

[1] It is this fact that I have tried to illustrate in my *Circumstances or Character?* (Methuen), 1911.

again, one way or the other, in strengthening or weakening the morale of the people, would at once make all the difference. At present nearly all the social work done owes its inspiration to Christianity. The workers are in the vast majority Christians, though often revolted Christians who repudiate the source of their convictions and have found other justification for them. This is clear in voluntary work, and, though the contention is harder to prove, it would seem to be the case in public service in state institutions.

III

Social and political movements.

The aim of life that each individual sets before himself tells not only in practical matters but also in the big social and political movements that are based on practical experience and guide the policy of their leaders. We are accustomed to the two broad divisions of temperament on which party government is based, but liberalism and toryism are not the real criteria by which the sheep among nations are divided from the goats. The real test lies in the answer to the question, ' Which come first : duties or rights ? self or others ? my class or the community ? ' On the right hand stands the conservative who wishes to save for the masses all the tradition of experience and culture that men have laboriously built up in the past ; and with him stands the liberal who is eager to secure for them all that the future may have in store and to secure it at once as soon as it may appear. While on the left stands the man who is the mere upholder of privilege, together with the man who is eager to grasp all he can secure by fair means or foul. The contrast is not between socialist and individualist, but between the men who insist on corporate obligation and individual duty on the one hand, and those who unite only to secure common advantages and insist on looking after ' number one ' on the other. The one lays stress on the rights of capital or labour as the case may be ; the other speaks of the responsibilities

of wealth and of the duty of honest work. The one seeks
to get, the other to give. The ideal of the one is the Super-
man, of the other the Man of Sorrows. The one goes the
way of the world ; the other treads the Royal Way of the
Holy Cross.[1] Christianity is the one philosophy that
insists on duties and has also power to bring parties nearer
to one another by uniting them in common work and
making them one in the Church.

Certain evils, it was made clear during the war, are so   Drink.
widespread as to threaten our national existence. The
seriousness of the problem of drink had long been recognized
by temperance reformers, and they had done much.
Drunkenness had ceased to be tolerated among the educated as it had been tolerated a century—or even a generation—ago. The middle classes were drinking less, and the
sordid customs of drinking in connexion with buying and
selling were growing daily more distasteful to the younger
and smarter men of business. Among artisans and labourers
there was much improvement : the cinemas had provided
a better form of amusement than the public house. Better
housing had notably diminished the evil. But still the
nation as a whole was strangely apathetic. A street crowd
continued to laugh at the disgusting spectacle of a drunken
man, and, in certain districts, to find amusement in the
sadder sight of a drunken woman. Drunkenness was still
one of the staple jokes of the music-hall and pantomime.
Among the class of manual workers occasional drunkenness
seemed to be considered no disgrace. Then we suddenly
woke up to the enormity of the evil. It threatened our

---

[1] à Kempis, *De Imitatione Christi*, Lib. ii, cap. xii ' Non est alia via
ad vitam, et ad veram internam pacem, nisi via sanctae crucis, et
quotidianae mortificationis. ' Et quomodo tu aliam viam quaeris,
quam hanc regiam viam, quae est via sanctae crucis ? '

(' There is no other way unto life, and unto true inward peace, but the
way of the holy cross, and of daily mortification. And how dost thou
seek any other way than this royal way, which is the way of the holy
cross ? ')

supply of munitions. It checked the building of ships. It kept back our coal. We realized something of the waste of drinking, the poverty it caused, the homes it broke up, the women it was leading to ruin, the children it made to suffer. We saw how soldiers were being robbed, and worse, under the influence of drink. Legislation was called for and proved of great effect. Y.M.C.A. and Church Army huts, concerts, boys' and girls' clubs, all set about counteracting temptation. But good as all this work was and is, it was merely external. To rely on it is to shirk the real issue. Ultimately the whole question is one of recognizing the obligation of self-respect and self-control.

Venereal disease.

Worse in character—and perhaps also in extent—are the ravages of venereal disease. The ' conspiracy of silence ' had left us ignorant of its awful consequences. We discovered that enormous as had been the improvement in the army since the repeal of the infamous Contagious Diseases Acts,[1] ten per cent. of the town population of England were suffering, many of them innocently ; [2] that more than half of the cases of blindness in children were due to the same cause ; [3] that its effects in causing nervous diseases, sterility,[4]

[1] During the thirteen years that these Acts were in force admissions to hospital in the Home Army increased from 210 to 260 per thousand. Since their abolition they have decreased from 270 to 66 per thousand. Other causes have, of course, co-operated in bringing about these results. For further information consult *Preventive Hygiene* : an account of the Brussels International Conferences, 1899 and 1902, and other publications to be obtained from The Association for Moral and Social Hygiene, 19 Tothill Street, Westminster, London, S.W.1.

[2] See the ' Final Report of the Royal Commission on Venereal Diseases, 1915 ', H.M. Stationery Office, Imperial House, Kingsway, London, W.C.1.

§ 46 : ' In a typical working-class population of London at least 8–12 per cent. of adult males and at least 3–7 per cent. of adult females have acquired syphilis. If congenital syphilis were included (and cases of gonorrhoea) . . . the proportion would certainly have been higher.'

[3] § 102 : 'The total percentage (of blindness in the London County Council schools) attributable to venereal disease was certainly 55·6, and may have been as large as 58·4.'

[4] § 101 : ' It is estimated that from 30 to 50 per cent. of sterility is due to this cause.'

paralysis, insanity,[1] and death,[2] were widespread.[3] Fortunately, wise and experienced men took the matter in hand. The discovery of remedies gave hope of checking the evil. It was realized that the former policy of assuming that a diseased person was guilty and of refusing treatment at general hospitals was wrong. It was cruel to the innocent. It led to concealment. It drove the ignorant to quacks. So the Government, acting through the Local Government Board, instructed county councils to supply free and systematic treatment, and itself met three-quarters of the cost. The county councils combined with the hospitals to make the necessary arrangements. The National Council for Combating Venereal Diseases undertook the preventive and educational side of the work in co-operation with schools, churches, and philanthropic agencies of all sorts, for it was felt that the causes of the evil must be attacked.[4] It remained for legislation to raise the age of consent and inflict heavier penalties on the organizers of the trade of vice. The London Council of Public Morality[5] co-operated with the police, approached music-hall and cinema proprietors who were generally anxious to do all they could to help, enlisted the help of workers in church and chapel. Women police and women patrols did splendid personal and individual work in helping and warning young girls in

[1] § 79 : ' Other forms of nervous disorder . . . are now known to be actually a late form of syphilis. " General paralysis " . . . is the most serious of them all. It is always a fatal disease which attacks either sex, in the prime of life (24–54 chiefly), and is responsible for 15 per cent. of male admissions to the asylums of large cities and nearly 3 per cent. of female admissions.'

[2] § 93 : ' In one series of 34 syphilitic mothers 175 pregnancies resulted in 30 apparently healthy children ; 104 died, and 41 were seriously diseased.'

[3] A synopsis of the Report is published by the National Council for combating Venereal Diseases, 80 Avenue Chambers, Vernon Place, Southampton Row, W.C.1. (1s. net.)

[4] See the various publications of the Council.

[5] 37 Norfolk Street, Strand, W.C.

moral danger in the parks and streets of London. The whole combined effort was entirely excellent and necessary in the face of the widespread organization of money-making prostitution.[1] But after all, all this good work—excellent as it has been—does not touch the real issue. The root of the whole evil is the anti-Christian teaching that man cannot be chaste, that chastity is injurious to health, that a man's health matters more than a woman's honour, that self-indulgence comes before self-respect, that if an evil cannot be entirely cured it is better to encourage it and make it as respectable and safe as you can—every item of which teaching is entirely and absolutely false. The fight in the last resort is between Christianity and Paganism.[2]

The 'native problem'.

The same contrast reappears in imperial questions. The ' native problem ' is, no doubt, a real difficulty in South Africa. The less developed black races are not able to assimilate European civilization in a single generation. No doubt they cannot be treated at once like white men. Their inability to govern or to maintain peace among themselves is the justification of our taking over the administration of their country. But the problem has been enormously complicated by the vice of white men. The half-caste population is not due to the violent passions of the negro but to

[1] Cp. Abraham Flexner, *Prostitution in Europe.* The Century Co., New York, for the Bureau of Social Hygiene, 1914, p. 190: ' Paris transactions are naturally on a far higher scale ; 200,000 and 300,000 francs (£8,000–12,000) have changed hands for a single business. Another establishment earned 70,000 francs (£2,800) for its owners in a single year. . . . Of 31 immoral resorts situated in the zone near the Arc the majority belong to the same managers.' P. 35 : ' The latest bordel of Budapest required an initial outlay of 500,000 crowns (£20,000) on which a very liberal return is expected.'

[2] See, for instance, the notorious passage in Lecky's *History of European Morals* (Longmans), 1877, vol. ii, p. 282, in which he glorifies the ' unhappy being whose very name it is a shame to speak, herself the supreme type of vice she is ultimately the most efficient guardian of virtue '. On p. 351 he rightly says that there is ' no other branch of ethics—which would be so deeply affected by ' the decay of dogmatic theology.

the deliberate sin of the self-controlled white man. Respect for the European races has been seriously undermined. A large amount of the popular prejudice against missions is due to the protests they have raised against the exploitation of the labour and honour of native races. Men have friends in South Africa who tell them that ' the missionaries are always causing trouble '. ' You talk like a damned missionary ' was the reply made by such a one to the suggestion that black men have rights.[1] Repression will never solve the problem. The remedy lies in education, in an education, that is, that believes in the ultimate equality of all men ; in other words, in religion that teaches that all men are sons of God. What this has done in Uganda is well known.

No less difficult is the problem of our Indian fellow subjects. Their country forms part of our Empire. They have been splendidly loyal. They bitterly resent our assumption of superiority, and naturally are offended at being classed with uncivilized Africans. They have a civilization older than ours, and regard us as discourteous and unmannerly, often not without reason. Our past attitude towards them has been full of ill-bred blunders, among which not the least has been the sending out of untrained and badly-educated missionaries to attack their beliefs. But the fact remains that, though the difference of East and West has been exaggerated, we are shirking the real issue if we ignore the differences of religion. There can be no real social intercourse or union of life between the liberty-granting and monogamous Christian and the Mohammedan whose creed countenances slavery and allows divorce and polygamy, none between the Catholic Church in which all are baptized in one body and kneel at one altar, and Hinduism with its system of caste and its sanction of consecrated prostitutes in its temples. A common faith in East and

East and West.

[1] *The East and the West*, January 1916, *The Position of Women in South Africa*, p. 65 : ' We complain of the problem of the coloured peoples (i.e. of half-castes), but the problem is entirely one we have brought on ourselves.'

West is the only power that can make the twain meet, and till India has contributed her interpretation of Christianity to the world, the Church remains imperfect, and Christ Himself is not fully revealed to men.

IV

The State and liberty.

These are great national and imperial problems, and they bring us to the greatest of all, the problem of government and the power of the State. They ultimately combine and concentrate in the problem of liberty to the forces of neo-paganism on the one side and the forces of Christianity on the other. In the externals of life, in individual men and women in social groups, the demand for liberty in art and education, in personal life and self-expression, in the right of corporate bodies as well as of individuals to exist as persons, is faced with the doctrine of the State as supreme.

Education.

This was the issue of the war. We have fought it out with Prussia. England is in little danger of allowing national art to be controlled by Parliament, and there are signs that reasonableness may be expected to prevail in the question of the school, for now that we have a minister of education appointed for his educational rather than his political qualifications there is every hope that liberty of religious teaching will not be denied to churchmen because one political party wants to thwart the Church, and the other to exploit her. We may hope to see Churchmen, Non-conformists, Roman Catholics, and Jews each encouraged to bring up their children in their own belief, in schools of their own, and taught by teachers of their own faith, with State help equally given to all.

The Marriage Law.

But the issue bids fair to come to a head over the law of marriage. The contrasts of the one side with the other are clearly marked. It is not merely that the institution of marriage itself is threatened by the advocates of divorce; that for the permanent union that owes its honour to its permanency they are opposing the conception of a terminable one. The precise conditions under which it is terminable do not touch the principle. Such unions, whether lasting for a few hours or for a lifetime, have always existed in the world but have been called by other, and less honourable, names.

But below the obvious question lie other considerations. The difference of a permanent relationship (other indeed, but in all that it involves at least as rich as that of blood relationship) from a mere contract, soluble at will, is clear. It is unnecessary to argue which is the higher. Further, a relationship involves the conception of duty and service; a contract is for mere mutual advantage. Duties never cease, even, to take the oft-quoted instance, towards an incurably insane person. If marriage is a mere contract Bertha Rochester should have been packed off to a State asylum, and Jane Eyre was a poor scrupulous fool. The question of the one and the many is equally involved. Advocates of divorce invariably argue from hard cases, regardless of the proverb about bad law. Ardent socialists will throw away all their convictions and declare that the interests of the community must be sacrificed to any girl who is dissatisfied with her husband, or to any husband anxious for a change. The question of progress or reaction is involved. Through nearly two thousand years the Church has worked her way towards her rule of monogamy, and has but hardly reached her goal. The Eastern Church allows remarriage in certain cases.[1] The Roman has strained the conception of nullity to breaking point. The English has been notoriously lax in keeping to her standards. The nominally Christian population has secretly gone back on Christian teaching; but at least there has been progress and such men have been ashamed of their deeds. The advocates of divorce wish to put back the clock nineteen centuries and to return to the paganism of the ancient Roman Empire.

It is not a question of State and Church, though the

The issues at stake.

[1] C. Gore, *The Question of Divorce* (Murray), 1911, p. 37.

liberty of the Church to call sin ' sin ' is threatened. It is not a question of laws of one body or another made for its own members. The Church does not make the law of marriage : she witnesses to it. It is eternal, in the nature of things as they are ' from the beginning '. The ultimate question, more important than all the above, because it includes them all, is this : ' Is there any such thing as right and wrong at all ? Is there any distinction between what is lawful and what is right ? Do morals depend on the chance vote of the majority of Parliament for the time being, and vary from country to country ? Can the State abrogate eternal laws of conduct ? Are we to render the things of God to Caesar or to God Himself ? '

Anti-Chris-
tian propa-
ganda.

A steady propaganda is being carried on in favour of Caesar's usurpation. It is organized in a society for divorce law reform, which deliberately seeks to influence public opinion by continual letters in the press. It is being helped unconsciously by writers of plays who have never thought out all that is involved, and possibly care more for striking situations than for the consequences of their action on public opinion. It is fostered by facile but confused thinkers who write novels, by authors who, without thinking at all, assume that a sentence in a court justifies a man in repudiating his wife and taking another woman in her place.[1] It is advocated by others who have deliberately defied the marriage law and equally deliberately try to undermine the belief of others in its authority, talking sometimes piously and sentimentally, but more often with fierce anger against Christianity and with bitter hatred of the Church.[2] Moreover, they have the advantage of being able to appeal to the baser instincts and passions of the natural man and are

[1] See above, p. 4, note 2.

[2] It is significant that the hero of Mr. Wells's story of the war, *Mr. Britling Sees it Through*, though he is intellectually converted to a sort of Manichaean Theism, shows no sign of moral conversion, or penitence for his sin with the eight women with whom he had committed, or played with, adultery.

sure of a wide response. It is true that the vast mass of people are still true to their marriage vows. The question is not yet the chief issue between the rival forces in society as far as the actual spread of divorce is concerned, but it is the one in which the contrast of the two ways is most clearly seen, where the greatest number of principles are involved, and where the two armies meet directly face to face. We have given the answer to Kaiserism in politics. It remains to give the same to Kaiserism in morals.

V

The Christian factor is the one that counts, in the external things of the world, in the individual, in corporate life, in the great struggle for liberty against the threatening power of the State. But to win the battle we need a Christianity that is sacramental, that sees that outward things are channels of the inward, material of spiritual, that can accept and hallow the exterior world, one that can strengthen and sanctify the individual, delivering him from narrowness, setting his feet in a large room, giving him freedom to expand in its atmosphere, to find his life in free self-expression, one mystical, internal, that gives communion with God in Christ ; we need a Christianity social, organized, institutional, one which is conscious of its continued corporate existence, in which one man can work with another, which as a whole is able to recognize the work of other social organizations, and to co-operate with them in their efforts ; we need one national that will interpret the people of England as a whole and at their best, that can meet our own peculiar wants and appreciate the Christianity of each other nations for its likeness and its differences. The English Church has a wonderful opportunity. As Protestant she has long ago repudiated the Kaiserism of Rome— a spirit in all other spheres hateful to the modern mind and discredited for all time to come ; as Catholic she can

The type of Christianity needed.

fulfil all the conditions and meet all the needs that we have been searching out. If only she can rise to her calling!

Much of what has gone before in the previous lectures may seem tedious and trivial. It may seem to deal with unimportant and petty matters of church life. It may seem of exclusively clerical interest, and it is, of course, primarily addressed to my fellow clergy. But, as we have abundantly learned, big issues depend on detail and on organization. The prime need in an army is the right training and the best education of the character of its officers.

The greatness of the task.

Life to-day, as we see it there outlying, is of intense interest. The world is full of the problems of its reconstruction after the ruin that we have seen. In the main the work must be done by the younger men, but by them in co-operation with the older, the repositories of tradition. We have lost many of those whose vigour and freshness was needed to take up the task. A heavy burden lies on us who have borne already much of the burden and heat of the day. But many are left who have had experiences that we others have never had, who as they heard the call to help England first in the battlefield of the trenches, have heard also the call to help her as soldiers of Christ. Καλὸν γὰρ τὸ ἆθλον καὶ ἡ ἐλπὶς μεγάλη.

REPRINTED ESSAYS

PASTORAL THEOLOGY AND ART

'What I am sure of is that it is Absolute Beauty that makes all things beautiful,' Plato, *Phaedo*, 100.

THE importance of the place of aesthetics in Pastoral Theology has been strangely overlooked. It has been almost ignored in books, and little less neglected in practice. The art of rhetoric, it is true, has received some study in its special application to the pulpit, and music and architecture have of necessity had their place in church life, but no one of these has been brought into close relation to any scientific consideration of the clergyman's work, while the minor arts, such as embroidery, decoration, metal and wood work, seem to be practised with hardly any consciousness that they are arts at all.

Yet, while truth speaks to the intellect of man, beauty calls out a response from his whole being. It is felt obviously by the emotions, but no less is the mind sensitive to the intellectual attraction of balance and harmony of ideas, and the heart recognizes at once the moral force of acts which are beautiful because they are well done. The bearing of art on Pastoral Theology is of immense importance if only because of its wide appeal, and it calls for study in all its several forms.

Art appeals to man through all his senses but especially through sight and sound. So the arts have been classified under the heads of painting, sculpture, architecture, and of music, literature, and oratory. A separate art, however, seldom stands alone ; so perhaps a better division to help us to judge of their place in Pastoral Theology would be one which starts from the attitude of the man concerned as passive or active. An art enjoyed passively whether by feeling or observing can often be isolated, and such are music and painting heard and seen by the ear and eye, but in an art pursued actively the will is called into play and there is generally some co-ordination of the different powers of the whole man ; voice and verse are united in song ; action and words are joined together in drama ; motion and sound are linked in the dance ; while music, speech, and movement, all three combine in opera.

I

What is the place of each of these in Pastoral Theology ? We may begin with the arts that appeal to the senses— painting and music—and consider them first as arts enjoyed passively. For practical religious life is little concerned with certain branches of aesthetics. It has little to do, for instance, with that which deals with natural beauty, except, perhaps, as it influences the choice of site for shrines and churches. Nor, again, has it much to say about the aesthetic appeal to senses other than those of sight or hearing. The sense of smell is approached in the use of incense, and scents have a wonderful power of recalling old associations and so ensuring stability and continuity of feeling by linking age to childhood in a bond of artificial piety, but even incense appeals as much to the eye ; at any rate its symbolism is drawn from the sight of its ascending clouds. The attraction felt by the Renaissance bishop for ' good strong thick stupefying incense-smoke ' was pagan rather than Christian, while touch and taste play practically no part in Christian worship whatever they may do in Hindoo or pagan religions.

The history of Christian art has been well studied, since most of our earlier Western art is Christian, and a tradition was established in the Middle Ages which lasted and survived through the Renaissance. Painting and sculpture, architecture as well as the minor arts, were of necessity connected with Christian life, so the study of their various forms has never been entirely dissociated from a consideration of their origins, their needs, and the purposes to which they were put. This has, perhaps, been specially the case with church-building and with the lesser arts, for you cannot study either a church, a chalice, or an illuminated manuscript, without some consideration of the people who went to the church, of the priest who used the chalice, or of the service which was read from the book. So, too, the question of the attitude of the Church towards art is generally at least referred to in standard histories, and we find in them fairly adequate treatment of such questions as the connexion of simplicity in early forms with the fear of persecution, the limits of syncretism with pagan elements, the connexion of iconoclasm with Eutychian heresy, the contrast of the public character of religious art in Italy with its domestic nature in Germany and Holland, of Michael Angelo and Raphael with Dürer and Rembrandt, or the hostility of Puritanism to art in church while often welcoming it outside.

But the more immediately practical questions of popularizing religious art in the present day and of employing its services for devotional or missionary purposes demand a much more thorough and scientific treatment than they have yet obtained. The use of the printing-press and of the various new processes of reproduction that have been invented ; the right balance and proportion in the use of various forms of decoration in churches ;[1] the best way to secure the building of fine churches and of making the most of those which we have ; the difficulty of making men realize that churches are offerings to God, and not buildings ' to seat 500 ' ; that there is all the difference between a war shrine ' erected to our heroic dead ' and something beautiful set up to the glory of God in memory of those who, like Christ, have given their lives for others ; the doctrinal change involved in this change of purpose ; the adaptation of church-building to modern conditions, to meet the needs

[1] At present stained glass is liked, people are mostly indifferent to decoration, plastic art is positively disliked, while architecture, though instantly appreciated when good, is little considered.

of choirs, of bicyclists, of class teaching, of parochial business, which can only be safely effected after the idea that
a church is primarily a place of worship has been firmly
established ; the relation of the new form of church to
national liturgical development ; these are all questions
of Pastoral Theology which should be thought out. The
mise en scène of ceremonial presented to the body of worshippers, as distinct from the taking part in it which is often
confined to a few, is also a matter of the art that appeals to
the eye. The interest in looking on which seems natural
to the Italian, as to Andersen's *Our Auntie*, with its sequence
of thought in image rather than word, is apparently growing
in English secular life, but the corresponding conception in
church life, with its corollary of worship by watching, at
present seems only to show signs of activity in irritation
and complaint.

In music, again, much has been achieved. There is a
strong tradition of religious music and a large stock of
works for use both in church and home. No history of
music can, or desires to, ignore the part the Church
has played in the growth of the art. Moreover there is
to-day a very close and practical relationship of music
to parish life ; and in connexion with church matters, considerable activity both mental and physical in the musical
world. The work being done by students of plain-song, the
efforts at reform made by individuals and societies, the
holding of conferences as well as the ordinary organization
of choir festivals and organ recitals, to say nothing of the
vast amount of painstaking labour on the part of organists in training choirs and of choristers in singing, all
witness to a widespread interest in the question of Church
music.

But much of the music produced is terrible rubbish, and
not a little in the worst possible taste. Much that is better
as music is extraordinarily unsuitable for the use to which
it is put. People are bored with long settings of the ' Te

Deum ' and of the ' Benedictus ' because the music even if good is often irrelevant. Bad traditions of former ages are firmly established. Our peculiar methods of chanting that so irritated Dvořák,[1] and our popular style of hymn that is the despair of our own masters, owe their origin to the two worst periods of English musical taste. Cathedral uses are applied by false analogy to parish churches. Foreign music written for a different and a Latin rite is ' adapted ' to our liturgy. Sometimes it is not even adapted and entirely new and ill-fitting words are set to Masses and ' Stabat Maters '. Mediaeval methods of chanting are revived with antiquarian exactness in spite of our changed conditions of custom and speech. The style suited to the drawing-room choral society is adopted for anthems and hymns. The tricks of the music hall and of the plantation melody are considered suitable for furthering the work of missions. All this has been allowed to grow up thoughtlessly in spite of the spiritual risks involved, in spite of the obvious discontent of the congregation, and in spite of the plain warnings of Church History that the whole matter bristles with difficulties.

Meanwhile the deeper problems connected with music have hardly been considered. Bad music makes it impossible for sensitive people to worship ; even inferior though good music is a hindrance to many who are specially susceptible to its influence or are accustomed to a high standard out of church, while to the unmusical even the best is mere noise. Obviously, alternatives of services with no music at all should be provided for these two classes. This is all the more necessary as the emotional power of music is very strong. Men, as more emotional, or perhaps as less self-controlled, seem to be more susceptible to its influence than

---

[1] Cp. C. V. Stanford, *Pages from an Unwritten Diary* (Arnold), p. 242 : ' Another distinguished visitor (to Cambridge) was Dvořák, who was nearly driven crazy by the chanting of the psalms, which he thought simply a barbarous repetition of a poor tune '.

K

women. Such a powerful influence is of very great account
in the moral question of the disciplining or the squandering
of the feelings. The use made of music in revival meetings
may possibly be working grave harm ; the preponderance
of musical sentiment in a race may be a source of serious
spiritual instability ; the excitement of patriotic sentiment
by really fine and obsessing national songs may play a large
part in hypnotizing a whole people to its moral and political
ruin.

The danger of dissociating music from meaning should
also be reckoned with. The harm of sacrificing sense to
sound is obvious even if it is not always remarked. It is
clearly spiritually harmful to get into the way of singing
words which we do not and cannot mean, because they are
joined to popular or even good music ; as Plato said, ' we
must compel the foot and the music to suit themselves to
the sense ' of a well-regulated and manly life, ' and not the
sense to suit itself to the foot and the music '.[1]   But there
is a further risk not so patent. Many men will come to
church to hear music because it commits them to nothing.
It involves no creed and entails no decision as to conduct,
while it satisfies the natural religious sentiment. They are
often in danger of turning to it as an anodyne for sorrows
that are meant to be a discipline. While some refuse to
face the problems of religion and turn to digging in their
gardens and, like Faust[2], find there the final word of
Wisdom, and others yield to an authority that claims in-
fallibility and trouble no more, so some take to music as a
substitute for religion. The danger of such ' art for art's
sake ' was seen long ago by St. Augustine, who weighed the

[1] *Republic*, Book III, 400 (tr. Davies and Vaughan).
[2] Part II.   Scene in the great Outer Court of the Palace :
Wie das Geklirr der Spaten mich ergetzt !

. . . . . .
Ja ! diesem Sinne bin ich ganz ergeben.
Das ist der Weisheit letzter Schluss.
Faust was, of course, only repeating Voltaire's conclusion put in the
mouth of Candide, ' Il faut cultiver nôtre jardin '.

value of church song against its risk,[1] and the contrast of music as rival to, or as servant of, Faith has been set out by Newman as perhaps only Newman could.[2]

On the other hand, if God is the source and ground of all beauty, there may well be a form of worship without words or even articulate thought, a form real even if lower, a sort of speaking in a tongue, or praying in the spirit, that is not incompatible with praying with the understanding also, one that consists simply in such communion with the eternal beauty that is God through the beautiful that is in earthly things.[3] If there is such a thing as art for art's sake it is either this or a thing that has nothing to do with Pastoral Theology at all.[4]

II

The same danger besets literary beauty. A writer may have a good style but nothing to say. A preacher may

[1] *Confessions*, Bk. X, ch. xxxiii ' Voluptates aurium tenacius me implicaverant et subiugaverant . . . Verum tamen cum reminiscor lacrimas meas, quas fudi ad cantus Ecclesiae tuae in primordiis recuperatae fidei meae, et nunc ipso quod moveor non cantu, sed rebus quae cantantur, cum liquida voce et convenientissima modulatione cantantur, magnam instituti huius utilitatem rursus agnosco. . . . Tamen, cum mihi accidit, ut me amplius cantus quam res, quae canitur, moveat, poenaliter me peccare confiteor, et tunc mallem non audire cantantem'.

[2] *Idea of a University*, Discourse iv. 6.

[3] Cp. Hooker, *Ecclesiastical Polity*, Bk. V, ch. xxxviii : ' In harmony the very image and character even of virtue and vice is perceived, the mind delighted with their resemblances, and brought by having them often iterated into a love of the things themselves. So that although we lay altogether aside the consideration of ditty or matter, the very harmony of sounds being framed in due sort and carried from the ear to the spiritual faculties of our souls, is by a native puissance and efficacy greatly available to bring to a perfect temper whatsoever is there troubled, apt as well to quicken the spirits as to allay that which is too eager, sovereign against melancholy and despair, forcible to draw forth tears of devotion if the mind be such as can yield them, able both to move and to moderate all affections'.

[4] Cp. R. W. Church, *Cathedral and University Sermons* (Macmillan), 1892 : *The Sense of Beauty a Witness to Immortality*.

have a gracious delivery but no message to deliver. There is a large number, too, of persons who love to sit and listen to the sound of words simply for their sound, who ask from them no meaning. This has a spiritually-weakening, or even deadening, effect. For :

' going over the theory of virtue in one's thoughts, talking well, and drawing fine pictures of it ; this is so far from necessarily or certainly conducing to form a habit of it in him who thus employs himself, that it may harden the mind in a contrary course, and render it gradually more insensible, i.e. form a habit of insensibility, to all moral considerations.' [1]

If this is true of the preacher himself, who must at least be mentally active, it is all the more true of the mere passive listener.

This danger of passivity is, however, less in oratory and literature than in painting and music. For words have meanings as well as sounds, and fail as words if they do not call forth active attention and thought, while action of any sort tends to involve the whole man and to combine his various faculties in exercise. So historically we find that literature arose from the drama and lyric. Action and words, or words and song, were first united ; only later, with their more conscious development, were they differentiated. For this reason writers on aesthetics have regarded drama as the highest form of art, a classification that seems a little unreal to us to-day when printing has become so common and has made our conception of literature one which depends so largely on the sight. Many people read almost entirely by the eye and hardly hear the sounds of what they read ; on the other hand, an aesthetic element has been added to literature in the form of good printing that makes a book ' a pleasure to read '. Still, even if the fact is not recognized, the inherited influence of drama and lyric lies behind all our canons of literary style.

[1] Butler, *Analogy*, ch. v. 2.

That there is beauty in speech has long been recognized, and the art of oratory has been well studied. The aesthetic pleasure of sound and of form has been analysed ; the study of phonetics and elocution have been pursued on the one side, while logic and rhetoric have examined scientifically the bases of that intellectual beauty that lies in ordered thought. They analyse what George Eliot called the ' exquisite kind of laughter which comes from the gratification of the reasoning faculties ',[1] and reckon with the laws which govern the grammar of assent. The value that style gives to Christian literature is familiar to all students of Augustine, Dante, à Kempis, Hooker, Pascal, Jeremy Taylor, or Newman, but perhaps it is less consciously recognized in prayer. Even though we speak of the Book of Common Prayer as a great English classic, and of our English Bible as ' living in the ear like a music that can never be forgotten ',[2] we probably little realize the value of both in continually lifting up our hearts into regions of fair conceptions to which we were otherwise incapable of attaining. The idea of worship by reading and hearing read, rising by a climax and turning to direct felicitous expression in prayer—the conception inspiring our English Matins and Evensong—is to our Church a possession of unique value.

Various problems in the combination of music and words are calling for study and solution. The recasting of plain-song built up originally to voice a liturgy in Latin so as to fit it to the genius of the English tongue with its so different accent and tone—a problem similar to that which the Western Church had to face when it adapted the Greek to the Ambrosian and Gregorian style of song ; the right language for hymns as lyrics—many of our present hymns seem to have been written only to read and are prosy ; their form and their number of verses—a comparison with the

[1] *Life*, vol. i, p. 165, quoted in R. H. Hutton's *Modern Guides of English Thought in Matters of Faith*, p. 270.

[2] F. W. Faber, quoted in J. Paterson Smyth's *How we Got our Bible* (Bagster), ch. vii.

living art of Welsh hymnody will show us that its metres are more varied than ours, and the verses rarely more than two or three ; the true relation of the speaking and the singing voice—our transitions from the one to the other are often grotesque in their contrast ; the part antiphonal-ism should play—as it played a part in the old Greek chorus ; the use of refrains—an almost universal feature of popular melody in folk-song and appearing in the responsorial singing of the Early Church ; the many questions of pitch and pace on which all massed singing depends for its magnificent effects ; all demand the attention of the student of Pastoral Theology.

Besides these there are all the many questions connected with the other language of gesture and action, of ceremonial as taken part in rather than as observed. Questions of dress, of the natural instinct for special vestments, be they chasubles or Geneva gowns ; questions of uniforms and their practical value to the wearers, be they monks or Salvation Army captains ; questions of well-established customs, such as wearing of mourning after a loss by death, or white at a first Communion, or of others, only beginning to obtain, such as the wearing of black in Holy Week or the increasing use of badges as indicating membership in societies ; all these as natural expressions of human life need to be examined sympathetically as to their spiritual import.

In ceremonial there must be a place for the working of the natural instinct of movement that finds expression in dancing, in drill and march, in swinging along the country roads in groups on bicycles, or threading the traffic in single file through the lighted streets on the return journey at the end of a summer day, or in playing football in a team that plays up and plays the game, sides backing up the centre and half-back supporting the forwards in perfect co-opera-tion. Some of these forms are accepted, others checked, in our Church. We are familiar with processions, but for simple votive offerings we make no provision. Pilgrimages have been transformed into outings and treats. Clapping of hands practised by the Therapeutae [1] in Egypt, and often seeking an entrance into church worship, seems now only to find a place in the Salvation Army use of the tambourine. ' Kneeling, crossing, holding up of handes, knocking upon the brest, and other gestures ' which the first Prayer Book of Edward VI said ' may be used or left as every man's devocion serveth without blame ', have long been left but are finding again their place in religious life. The natural free grouping of congregations that forms such an attractive feature in foreign churches is forbidden to us by our stiff and ugly arrangement of seats. We have practically no religious drama—to our great loss, as visitors to Ober-Ammergau will have realized—and we are not likely to have this, almost the highest form of religious art, till the human interest of action is allowed to have more free play in church and to be sanctified by us in worship.

For all liturgical worship is dramatic. The aesthetic principles of liturgiology need emphasizing. As a drama has a beginning, a middle, and an end, so there is a definite proportion between the different elements in the Eucharist or Choir Office. The varying parts of the service on any one day are built up on lines familiar to the student of liturgiology as the musical sequence in a Latin Mass of Introit, Kyrie, Gloria, Credo, Sanctus, Benedictus, and Agnus Dei is familiar to the musician.[2] Public worship is a drama, or rather opera, a work in which all take part, and

[1] Philo, *de Vit. Cont.* 484. 33, ed. F. Conybeare, who gives other references.

[2] The sequence of the English Liturgy is somewhat different as the Gloria comes at the end. This is probably the reason why in services adapted from the Latin, or written by English composers who know the old tradition by study and never worship in the church of their own homeland, the Glorias are so unsuitable. A similar sequence of narrative, meditation and chorus, and choral forms the structure of Bach's great Passion Music.

with its scope for combining music, speech, and action is the highest art of which man is capable.[1]

III

The chief value of the study of the connexion of Pastoral Theology and Art lies in the service such a study renders to religion, but the services it would render to Art are in their way no less. The world as well as the Church would gain by a closer co-operation of the two.

The necessity of religion for any great Art has been ably argued by Ruskin and by many other writers. It is as an active stimulus that it is required rather than as a restraining power. The element of discipline is no doubt necessary, but possibly it is because this side has been over-empha-sized that the Church has been regarded by many as a hindrance to the free play of artistic powers rather than as a source of inspiration. Still there has been, as a matter of fact, a definite Christian contribution to the world's wealth of beautiful things, and *Old Pictures in Florence* have not merely taught Art to ' fold her hands and pray ' but also to ' paint man, man, whatever the issue ' and ' to bring the invisible full into play '. Few artists will endorse Professor Haeckel's suggestion that the place of Christian Art can be taken by microscopic enlargements of the anatomy of beetles and butterflies and that the lower groups of plants and animals will afford a satisfactory

[1] G. Lowes Dickinson, *Religion : A Criticism and a Forecast* (Brimley Johnson), 1906 : ' Ritual is, or should be, a product of two of the greatest arts, literature and music, with the assistance, perhaps, of an element of drama. . . . For those who can accept the Christian view the Christian ritual must be their most precious possession . . . and if, as I think will be the case, the men in whom the religious instinct is strongest move farther and farther from the Christian postulates, a ritual which shall express their new attitude will become, perhaps is already, one of their chief spiritual needs '. Of the High Churchmen who have had not a little success in evolving such a ceremonial the author speaks with a special bitterness.

'inspiration for painting, architecture, and technical art' (at any rate to any one but a German professor) even if they afford one ' entirely new '.[1]

To-day also the Church remains, for good or evil, the chief popular school of Art. To the masses the religious pictures in their cottages stand for high art, as contrasted with photographs of relatives the interest of which is personal rather than aesthetic. The general absence of feeling for plastic art, as shown, for instance, in the public monuments of London, is probably directly traceable to the successful Calvinistic hostility to images. The low standard of English popular music, in spite of the musical capacities of the people, is, it may be, directly traceable to the long-continued opposition of Puritanism to music in church even if it encouraged it outside. Here the results are more conspicuous as the people will have music of some sort in their worship. The efforts of those who are working for the cause of good music apart from Church music are comparatively ineffectual, as to the great mass of people pure music without song or some other interest seems futile, as purposeless as mere decoration without something to decorate. For them this interest will be found either in religion or amusement. The Church as a great popular school of music is the only really effective barrier to the influence of the music-hall melody, since the influence of the government school ceases with boyhood.[2]

[1] *Die Welträtsel*, Kap. xviii, tr. J. McCabe, p. 121.

[2] Cp. M. W. Keatinge, *Studies in Education* (A. and C. Black), 1916, p. 101 : ' Unless moral training and the sense of social responsibility bulks as big as aesthetic training, unless, indeed, the two are merged into one, the training of the feelings on which so much stress has been laid may be disastrous. . . . When the Church was the guardian of fine art and of knowledge, the moderating influence of fine art was always present. Unfortunately the gulf between the Church and aesthetics is now very wide, and there is a danger that both clergy and teachers, apart from certain technical qualifications, may become markedly less cultured than other professional men of ability. When this happens, organization is of no avail and education is fraudulent.'

How close is the connexion between the Church and the musical world can be seen by looking at the advertisements of any musical paper or publisher's catalogue. Professional musicians are largely church organists and choristers who play and sing for a livelihood, and their teaching connexion often depends on their appointment. As a consequence the relations of the clergy and organists are continually strained. Moreover, in music the second rate is in possession by a long tradition. Musicians are in special danger of narrowness in outlook since music does not necessarily demand any definite connexion with thought or literature or general culture, and, as we saw, only that conception of beauty is fertile which grasps life as a whole. So it comes about that the market is flooded with silly oratorios and with ' easy and effective music '. Bishop Creighton, after enjoying ' a fine anthem of Pergolesi ' at the Temple Church, complained that ' elsewhere he was persecuted with Stainer, &c.' [1] Meanwhile our better musicians, instead of writing for actual needs, compose Masses to Latin words (not being themselves Roman Catholics) and wonder that the critics find them academic and uninspired. Much steady work for reform is, no doubt, being done, but for success it must be based on popular life. We are told that Russian music is largely the outcome of training of the people in Church music, and the same training must be secured in England if the future of music of our people is to be inspired.

It is, however, in Architecture that our artistic failure is most conspicuous, perhaps because of the contrast of its early greatness. Here we find the same academic unreality. ' From here,' said an architect of a new Roman Catholic church, ' you can see five altars.' But who, except the penitent of Pascal's Jesuit,[2] ever wants to see five altars at

[1] *Life*, vol. ii, p. 270.

[2] *Lettres Provinciales*. Neuvième lettre. ' De là je conclus que vous pouvez ouïr la messe en très peu de temps, si, par exemple, vous rencontrez quatre messes à la fois qui soient tellement assorties, que, quand l'une commence, l'autre soit à l'évangile, une autre à la consécration et

once ? The architect, an agnostic of Baptist extraction, evidently regarded them as mere pieces of ornamentation. Moreover, such failure is not remedied by tests. In this case it was made a condition that the architect was to be a Roman Catholic, but the man appointed was ' ghosted ' by the agnostic in question. The only remedy lies in a continued and general bringing together of the architectural and ecclesiastical world. Till this is effected we shall have no satisfactory development of church architecture. Churches that are to be filled with seats will be designed without them ' because an empty church makes such a much better drawing '. The same old mediaeval plans will be repeated. Mean churches will be built ' to seat ' so many. The tension between clergy and architects will continue unrelieved.

But besides such co-operation we need a change of idea ; we need to recover the conception of a church as a place of worship. We must make a careful study of the intimate connexion of liturgiology and church building. We must secure a full realization on the part of architects of the use to which a church is to be put, and an equally full realization on the part of the clergy of the inner spiritual value of a beautiful church, and the bar to spiritual growth that is presented by a bad one—a hindrance all the more serious because, fixed by wood and stone, it is continuous and unalterable.

In literature we find the same story of national opportunities missed. Even in sermons, which should be setting a standard of artistic speech and pronunciation to the people, we find slipshod grammar and careless articulation. Many of our hymns are below the level that would be accepted in a child's school recitation book. The reading

la dernière à la communion. . . . Certainement, mon Père, on entendra la messe dans Notre-Dame en un instant par ce moyen. Vous voyez donc, dit-il, qu'on ne pouvait pas mieux faire pour faciliter la manière d'ouïr la messe.'

of the lessons often shows an entire lack of sense of the beauty, or even the meaning, of what is read. The idea of worship of the mind seems to be held of little value, and the consequent loss to the nation's thought and literary sense is incalculable.

Yet what the Church might be giving is so needed in the literature of to-day. Apart from the deliberate immorality of many of the best written novels, the cult of ugliness in much modern poetry and drama prevents it from rising to greatness. Even in some of the best there is something wanting, a lack of a sense of beyond, a depressing limitation of outlook that calls aloud for the truth which sets us free.[1]

Beyond all the recognized forms of art remains the social artistry of manners. The moral beauty of a life well lived works out in gentleness and breeding of dignity of behaviour. Enormously as our people are increasing in refinement there is still much to wish for. Gracious and attractive as is English civilization as seen at its best among English gentlemen and gentlewomen, it cannot be said yet to be evolved to the full or diffused through the whole people. There is much in the language and bearing in our ' middle ' and ' lower ' classes of which we must feel ashamed. Yet the Church is the one refining influence available for all and at all times, and the one that can give an adequate motive both for the rough to strive towards better things, and for the cultured to give of their best, and to give themselves to the less fortunate in daily intercourse with their fellow men.

[1] Even such a fine poem as the often-quoted sonnet of Rupert Brooke's, beginning ' If I should die think only this of me ', might have been so far greater if it had been inspired by the Christian hope of Resurrection instead of the unsatisfying Pantheism that seems to others beside Tennyson (*In Memoriam*, xlvii) to be a ' faith as vague as all unsweet '.

IV

The work to be done is enormous. The Church fails to reach the masses of men to-day, yet Art, her most powerful missionary ally, is almost ignored. ' If the Eastern peoples,' writes a Japanese Buddhist, ' were shown the artistic side of Christianity, and began to talk with pious Christians heart to heart through art, they would be far more ready to appreciate Christianity than the experiences of missionaries have led them to expect.' [1] The hero of Huysmans' *En Route* was led back to Christianity by the music and devotion he found in the Paris churches ; where is the church in London to which an English Durtal could go and find himself led to Christ by the beauty of the chanting and the sense of the presence of God ? Our missionary exhibitions show hideous photographs of converts in surplices and beautiful pictures of pagan rites, without realizing how they are thwarting their own efforts. There is little use made of the appeal from beauty in apologetics either in formal works or in practical evidential preaching, yet it is her heritage of living beauty that attracts to the Church of Rome every day men who have no real desire to be dominated by a foreign prelate. Our knowledge of ' the one eternally satisfying answer to all the questions that could ever be asked ' too often have to be symbolized, as to the Indian officer of Mr. E. F. Benson's *Arundel*, by objects as unlovely as the ludicrous image of ' the regimental church, with its pitch-pine pews, its crude windows, its encaustic tiles, and its braying harmonium '.

[1] *The Hibbert Journal*, vol. iv, October 1905, *How Christianity appeals to a Japanese Buddhist*, by M. Anesaki, Professor of the Philosophy of Religion in the Imperial University of Japan. The whole article is most interesting, and not the least interesting passage is one which shows how the conscience of the East was shocked by the action of the German Emperor in ' stimulating his soldiers to commit murder for revenge, so that the peoples of the East might remember for a thousand years the terrible vengeance of Christians '.

The strength of the artistic appeal is not only great in itself, but also from the fact that its force is felt quite independently of education. Argument has little effect even on the educated and still less on the mass of men, while art appeals to all. But so far are we from using it that we actually allow bad art to alienate men who are leaders of modern thought. ' From the end of the vast cold space,' writes one, ' came the dreary wail I remembered so well. I had heard Church music in Moscow and knew what it ought to be.' [1] It is quite wrong, surely, that church-going should be regarded as a bore, yet such was the case when Dr. Johnson lamented that he failed to take pleasure in public worship,[2] and such is almost invariably the case to-day. The power of literature is greater than either painting or music ; the written word penetrates where the voice of the preacher cannot go. It is difficult to believe that any Jew would be converted by our modern preaching methods ; it is little probable that he would be won by Church music ; the conversion of Israel will far more probably come when, having accepted Christian ethics and the Christian outlook on life, the Chosen People begins to seek for its bases and finds it through the channel of Christian literature.

But for literature to be useful for missionary purposes it must be such that men will read it again and again. Yet how extraordinarily little theological writing there is that is worth reading for its style ; how few books that rise to being literature. Shorthouse's *John Inglesant* has probably done more to make men understand and love the English Church than any ten volumes of Divinity. Our great need to-day is of Christians who can write and so to beat neo-paganism on its own ground in magazines, in the daily press, and in novels, men who will satisfy those who are

[1] *Appearances*, by G. Lowes Dickinson (Dent), 1914.
[2] *Prayers and Meditations*, April 9, 1773, ' I hope in time to take a pleasure in Public Worship '.

determined to live resolutely in the universe of all that is fair and good.[1]

The work to be done is both theoretical and practical. On the side of theology we want a much fuller study of the theology of art. We want to show how Christian philosophy, with its fuller understanding of human nature, is better equipped for interpreting its character. We want a working out of its place in Christian apologetics, of its relation to morals, whether subordinated as by Plato, or co-ordinated as each an end in itself, of the connexion of its forms in worship and in life, of its place in education as a whole and as an instrument in the education of the individual.

We want, too, a further study of the psychology of art as an active expression of human nature and of its consequent place in religious life. We want to separate the idea of religious art from the Latin spirit with which it is often confused, and to show that its place in worship is the outcome of a Catholic instinct, independent of the military and legalizing spirit of Roman Christianity. We want to study this human instinct in its actual expressions to note what is universal and what is peculiarly English, as a preliminary to the practical work of reviving Catholic customs and developing those which are peculiarly our own.

Then the various tasks that are seen to be demanded can be taken in hand. We can set about creating schools of Church music, of painting, of embroidery. We can utilize our magazines, our printing press, our reproducing processes. We can form societies for producing church ornaments, and guilds for designing monuments. We can take up the task of Christianizing and so beautifying our churchyards and cemeteries. We can carry on our propa-

---

[1] Cp. Goethe, *Generalbeichte* :

'Uns vom Halben zu entwöhnen,
Und im Ganzen, Guten, Schönen,
Resolut zu leben.'

' Vivre au grand jour ' is said to have been Comte's motto. Cp. Leslie Stephen, *English Thought in the Eighteenth Century,* vol. ii, p. 278.

ganda through shops; we can set about the work of restoring churches, of clearing them of the heavy blocks of seats that interfere with free motion, and covering their bare walls and filling their empty niches.

But all this must be done in consultation with experts. We must so organize that artists of all sorts may be in touch with the clergy and understand each other's points of view. By conferences, by Summer Schools, by Guilds and Associations, by interchange of opinion in the professional organs of our several callings, by personal and social intercourse, we must do all we can to secure the co-operation that is so sorely needed.

THE WELL-ORGANIZED PARISH

A CANDIDATE for Orders seeking a title, or a curate who has to find a new post, naturally wishes to find out all he can about the parish he thinks of going to, before making any decision. But, as a rule, when he goes to interview his vicar that may be, he is quite at a loss to know what to look out for and what to ask. The result is that his inquiries generally reduce themselves to questions about ritual and to finding out if he will have one day off in the week. And, as he does not wish to give the impression that he is superficial or slack, he does not like to ask too much even on these points.

Yet it is a serious matter. In any profession so much depends on the first start, but with a clergyman the issue is more grave as a demand is made on his whole life. A great deal of unreal language is often used about the claims of clerical duty—in many points, perhaps, they are no different from those of any other calling, but it is a peculiar fact that all that a parson does counts, whether professionally or unprofessionally; he is always on duty except when definitely away on a holiday; he becomes part of the local life of a parish; his profession lays its claims on the whole man; and, therefore, just as a clear understanding is all the more necessary when a man does business with his relations, so between curate, vicar, and parish, it is important to have the position clearly understood from the first.

The extent of these claims and their results in the lives of those under authority seem to be hardly recognized by the beneficed. Their memories are very short, as people naturally like to forget troubles. The causes of their own discontent in former days were not generally thought out, and, being merely impressions, they passed away with the conditions that caused them. They bemoan the scarcity of curates, and wonder what its cause may be, while the language of their plaint does much to explain the cause. Meanwhile the curates are unvoiced ; they have no consti- tutional means of stating how and where the present system galls them ; they perhaps cannot suggest how it may be improved and do not care merely to complain, especially since, as a rule, their vicars are personally almost too considerate and kind. They allow them anything except a position. So, many turn away from the priesthood, both before and after Ordination.

But it is not merely the status of the unbeneficed that depends on a clear understanding of what is wanted ; the question is part of the much larger one of the nature of church work. Vicars complain that men who apply to them (it was a vicar's wife in the particular case I have in mind) only want Sunday duty—though that means less than a living wage. Obviously their faith in the Church is not at fault—her common worship is a fact and her pulpit is a power—but about the ' parish work ' that represents her activities during the week, they have their doubts. Therefore the various points that the applicant for a curacy should ask are worth thinking out, as they will suggest various much needed reforms in matters which press especially heavily on the unbeneficed, and in the present dearth of curates to raise the question of these reforms will do much to bring them about. It is not suggested that the applicant should bargain for their concession—it is not his place to set his superiors right—but he may fairly give his preference to a place where things are more satisfactory, and this, under present circumstances, would be a strong inducement to the curateless to ask themselves why they cannot get help, and so become a strong lever to raise the whole conception of parish work.

In going to see the vicar of his proposed new parish the candidate should look out for definite points rather than mere impressions. He should consider in each department of the work what is wanted in principle, and should look for the signs which will show if it is there. The features of parish life may be arranged in the following order :

(1) The spiritual life of the parish must be the basis of all. If this is sound all the rest can be mended and reformed, or, at the worst, endured. If it is not the case is hopeless. The spiritual life of a church centres in the Eucharist, whether, as by one school, it is made prominent and familiar as the chief act of worship, or, as by another, guarded with reserve. An experienced priest once gave a young curate, who was thinking of going to another parish, the advice, ' See if his celebrations are right. If they are, all the rest will be.' He disregarded the advice given him (the altar linen was dirty and the vessels were put away without being properly cleansed), and was sorry for it afterwards.

The candidate should ask if the Eastward or the North end position is taken. There is a place for both uses in the Church of England, but there can hardly be a place for priests holding opposite views on the subject in one parish. He should ask if he is expected to duplicate (except in cases of sickness or accidents), if he is expected to do so normally, if regularly in the holiday time ; he should find out if the church work is built up on the assumption that one member, or more, of the staff does so, and should decide within himself whether he considers this to be right. He should ask how often he is expected to celebrate, and should find out if celebrations are unnecessarily multiplied on every special occasion. He should notice the altar linen to see if it is clean and if there is the proper supply. He should observe the whole sacristy arrangements, whether the vessels are properly washed, by whom they are handled, how far silence is observed by the celebrant both before and after the service, whether there is a sacristy distinct from the choir vestry.[1] Especially where there are late celebrations

---

[1] Where there is only one vestry the celebrant may sometimes vest and prepare the vessels quietly in the church itself or in a side chapel.

he should ask if the celebrant is allowed to keep to himself before approaching the altar, or if he will be expected, say, to take a class in the Sunday School. He should notice if the vicar talks to the choir and churchwardens right up to the beginning of the service and begins again as soon as he has left the altar. He should observe whether the congregation remain in the church to say their thanksgiving, or if the verger turns them out by noisily opening the door directly the clergy enter the vestry.

These things are some of them small, but the smallest are indications of things of primary importance. In connexion with these the general church arrangements should be noticed, whether there are seats or chairs, whether they are fixed or loose, whether there is room for the congregation to kneel, whether the church is clean, whether there are kneelers in the side aisles or whether ' the quality ' alone are expected to say their prayers on their knees.

(2) The next point is that of finance. Bad finance affects everything else, and forms an insuperable bar to reform in more spiritual matters. The candidate should find out if the account-keeping of the parish is careful, and if the financing of the work is sound.

He should inquire, therefore, if a complete statement of accounts is published and should ask to see it. It will further serve to give a clue to all the activities of the parish. He should notice if it is inclusive, if properly audited, if the separate accounts are really kept separate, and separately balanced. He should ask if he may see the books, and should notice whether they are kept in the vestry, how the money is entered, whether it is paid into the bank regularly every week, how many different accounts there are at the bank.

He should find out how the money is raised, whether by collections in the church alone, by special appeals, by bazaars, by systematic subscriptions, or by pew rents. If by the latter, he should consider whether, under such circumstances, it is possible for the church life to be healthy, and should ascertain if any real attempt is being made to get rid of them. He should ask if there is any finance committee or Church Council, how far it accepts responsibility, how far it has any real control of the funds. He should discover to what extent the minor funds are separately financed, and have treasurers of their own, and how far they meet their expenses.

He should know if the church is in debt, and how far general church expenses are covered. He should find out if he will be able to get money for general expenses, and how far he will be expected to pay for things out of his own pocket (e.g. postage, confirmation manuals, &c.), if he is expected to subscribe to clubs, &c., and to how many, if he will have to give back part of his salary at every church collection. He should find out if the vicar pays for things out of his own pocket ; if he does so deliberately in order to keep everything in his own hands ; what is the course adopted when any one wishes to propose some action that may involve expense.

(3) Good finance is usually a sign of system in general. The candidate should try to find out how far the work is done by method ; how far the government of the parish is constitutional so that there is a proper time and place for everything ; how far things are done in co-operation and after consultation with others, in the way that is recognized as necessary in business or in the management of societies ; how far each worker has his sphere defined in itself and in relation to the whole, or how far the work is ' personal ' and direct, originating from the vicar alone ; how far the assistant clergy are mere ' handymen ' doing odd jobs and entrusted with no real responsibility.

He should therefore ask if there is a Church Council, how often it meets, what are its powers and constitution. He should find out whether it is merely consultative, whether the vicar acts as it advises, whether its members attend, whether it has any actual powers, how far it has any financial control in the parish, what is its relation to the district visitors. He should ask how it is formed, whether nominated or elected ; if the latter, whether the qualification to vote is that of being a communicant, or paying money in any way ; whether women vote for, and have seats on, the Council.

He should find out how things are arranged ; whether individuals approach the vicar, or bring matters up for consideration at the Council ; what is the staff of church workers, whether Mrs. Pardiggle is among them and how many of her there are ; how far the various organizations are independent with committees of their own ; what they are, and how far they are co-ordinated ; whether their representatives meet one another, whether, e.g. the Sunday School teachers know the week-day school teachers ; whether any one interest is prominent (music, missions, clubs, &c.), and if it is so to the detriment of others.

(4) The above points will be difficult to find out, as the effectiveness of organizations can only be known from inside. But whether they are effective or not will depend on the methods of the staff, that is, ultimately, on those of the vicar.

The candidate should therefore find out what these are ; whether they are ' personal ' and centre in his study, the church documents, perhaps even the accounts, being kept there. If this is the case, every matter will have to be talked over and settled by the direct method of conversation. Few records will be made in writing and there will be little continuity in the work. If his methods, on the other hand, are orderly, everything will tend to centre in the church, the vestry will become the office for the staff, the common ground where its members can meet at definite hours. Their professional work will thus be kept separate from domestic life to the greater purity and vigour of both.

The candidate should therefore ask if the church is kept

open, and should find out to what extent the clergy can be seen there at definite times ; whether people who want their services have to ring a front door bell and be shown into the dining-room ; whether there is a proper vestry or only a shed where cassocks and surplices are hung ; if there is not, whether there is any scheme on foot for building one. He should ask what records are kept other than the registers demanded by law ; to what extent the vestry is an office, the church a common meeting ground where the clergy meet together for common prayer.

He should find out how the work is arranged, whether haphazard or on some plan, whether it is settled for a week in the vicar's study on Monday morning ; or whether there is any system fixed for once and for all to allow of more continuous action, with such modifications from time to time as may be necessary. He will know if the vicar is married and should notice whether his wife is continually in and out of his study, and whether she talks parish shop at meal-times.

(5) On the methods of the vicar will depend the whole style of the work, whether it is amateur or thorough, how far it will be such as a self-respecting man can do. The candidate should have in his mind some lay friend, and should imagine him asked to conduct his business by the methods accepted in parish work. The standard should be at least as high as that of lay work, though the candidate will have to put up with less. If, however, he sees a chance of working for reform this will not matter, but if it fails altogether to stand the test, he is, if he accepts the curacy, preparing for himself a future of acute unhappiness.

He should therefore ask if there are day schools in the parish in which a religious education is given by trained teachers. He should find out how often the clergy teach in them ; to what extent they take an interest in the whole work of the teachers ; how far the schools are made the centre, after the church, of the whole work of the parish. He should ask if there are Sunday Schools or if there is a Children's Service or Catechism instead. He should visit both week-day and Sunday Schools or service, and see how the discipline and teaching of the latter compares with that of the former ; if it is unsatisfactory he should find out what steps are being taken to improve it and if anything is being done beyond mere talking.

(6) If the standard of work is high the church will be respected. The sign of this will be found in the extent to which it is in touch with the neighbourhood, or how far it is merely parochial. The candidate should, therefore, find out what inter-parochial activities there are, how far the clergy are in touch with their fellow clergy, in what diocesan movements the congregation takes part, which it supports, what special interests it has (e.g. missions, church extension, education, social work). He should find out how far the clergy are in touch with Nonconformists, with local life, what part as churchmen members of the congregation take in public service, as Guardians, Councillors, Organizers of Charity, &c., how far the church is represented in the local Press.

He should consider whether this is overdone, and whether the activities of the church are not too secular. He should notice the vicar's books in his study, to gather how far he is a student and if he is in touch with the best theological, and other, thought.

(7) If this extra-parochial activity is really a spiritual force, the functions of the church and secular life, though closely related, will be clearly defined and fully differentiated. If there is reliance on material means for spiritual ends they are bound to fail. Bribery cannot convert a man, and an ' institutional ' church is a substitute for, not an aid to, religion.

The candidate should therefore find out what line is adopted for the work of charity. He should notice what sum is spent on relief of the poor, and should ask how it is administered, whether by the vicar at his own personal discretion, or by a committee considering each case after careful inquiry and on its merits. He should find out if such a committee is a real committee with a proper lay and masculine element, how far its decisions are binding and control the relief given, or if it is a mere meeting of the vicar and district visitors to report what they have done already. He should find out how far the alms are administered on any plan or if mere doles are given, how far with real knowledge of those in distress or of social conditions, or haphazard and on impulse.

He should find out how far a system of reliance on material means runs through the work ; how far Sunday Schools and Bands of Hope are kept alive by treats, or mothers' meetings by subsidized clubs ; whether slate clubs are being run ' to get hold of the men ', and—this is the point—what steps are being taken to emancipate the church from this bad tradition. He should try to gauge the whole attitude adopted towards the poor, whether it is one of patronage, either direct, or that involved in an unnatural assumption of equality ; or whether demands are made on them and Christianity represented as a religion of the Cross.

(8) Personal considerations may be left to the last. If in the above points the work is right the candidate need not fear that he will be unreasonably treated. It should be clearly understood that he will have one day off in the week, sleeping out of the parish one night if he wishes ; he should get settled what holiday he may expect, and he may give full weight to the important question of his own salary.

It is not to be expected that everything will be perfect in all these points. ' Do not hope for Plato's Republic,' wrote Marcus Aurelius to himself, ' suffice it if the smallest thing makes head ; to compass that one issue, believe, is no small feat.'

MOTHERS' MEETINGS

It had always seemed to me that in our work amongst 'the poor' we make the mistake of doing what we think they must like, instead of asking ourselves what, as a matter of fact, they appreciate ; that we start organizations on the assumption that they must do good, instead of finding out how they strike those whom they are intended to benefit. It must surely be better to educate the conceptions of right and wrong which such persons already have than to force on them our methods, which, from their point of view, may be positively bad.

At the same time, feeling that I had no positive knowledge that we were doing so, I determined to test the matter in the case of some recognized branch of church work. I knew that the clergy felt an unconquerable distaste for mothers' meetings, which might be due to an instinctive feeling of their inutility, and that it was the custom of working-class boys, whenever they saw a knot of women talking together, to jeer at them as ' a mothers' meeting ', so I determined to take the opinion of them held by such persons of the working-class as I might come across casually, when engaged about the house, in trains, or elsewhere. The two questions I tried to put were—What is your opinion of mothers' meetings ? What is the general opinion of them as you have heard it ? The answers are given below, as far as possible in the actual words of their replies.

1. A reservist, engaged as a rough porter in a block of buildings, said :

My wife goes to one, and I'm sure all she hears there is good. People talk about them, but then there are people who always say people go to church for what they can get, and accuse others.

11. An assistant-teacher, however, answered :

Oh ! I don't know ; they're all right for some people, but I don't hold with them. Nine times out of ten they go for what they can get—I don't mean the good they can get. I've heard a good deal about them ; some of the biggest hypocrites go, and get all sorts of things. There was a girl whose mother used to go all across London to one, as well as to one here, and she said to me, 'There's nothing to be lost by it, you know, Miss.'

12. An engineer gave as his opinion :

It all depends how they are managed. They are too denominational, as a rule. My mother used to work for one, and there was too much for those who went to church. I think they are good where they are worked by clubs, and by being able to buy things at a cheaper rate. The general opinion is that people don't think much of them, that they are only places for gossip ; but I don't agree with that. I think they might be some good, but, as it is, those who plead the most get most benefit. The cases ought to be searched into, and not taken in the way they do. Several I know have had things offered to them because they are naturally decrepit-looking. But I don't know much about them. I can't say they do much harm.

13. A teacher in an evening school volunteered :

I hate these mothers' meetings. It depends, of course, on the women who take them, but I think all the scandal of the parish is talked over in them. Perhaps that is a bit drastic, and I've been only in one place for so long.

14. A treasurer of a friendly society said :

My mother said she would never go to one as long as she could get a penny any other way. She used to say she would have liked to go if it weren't for the things they give away there. She only went once and—well, she isn't one who objects to a woman having a glass now and then, but as for the woman she sat next to ! However, the lady didn't seem to notice it.

Some of the women used to go to two or three. She formed her opinion of them from the women who used to attend. They used to come to her, and offer to sell the things they had just been given, saying, ' I've such a nice little cloak the lady has given me.' They wanted the money to get drink with.

15. A furniture-remover gave as his opinion :

I think they are quite unnecessary. If they go for spiritual benefit they could get it just as well at church, and would have no need to neglect their homes. I think that is the general opinion, too. I was working the other day with four married men, and they said when they saw a meeting going on, ' There's a fine thing. That is what they call looking after their homes.' And they were the class of men who meant what they said, and didn't just say it to be clever.

Before drawing any conclusion from these replies, three things must be taken into consideration. I tried to make my questions colourless, often saying first, ' I want to ask your opinion, but please say just what you think, not what you think I want you to say.' But, of course, the mere fact of the question being asked gave a lead in one direction, as no one who believes thoroughly in an institution asks questions about its utility, and every one who is accustomed to dealing with uneducated people knows how prone they are to give the answer that is expected of them. Again, allowance must be made for a natural tendency to criticize, and especially to run down church work to a clergyman, when an opportunity presents itself. A man with no particular knowledge or opinion of his own would be sure to speak disparagingly of mothers' meetings to me. The temptation to assume airs of superiority in answering my questions must have been almost irresistible.

Once more, we must remember the natural selfishness of a large number of men, who grudge their wives any relaxation, and expect them to be slaves in their homes. As long as the working-classes ignore the claims of their wives to rest and change on Sunday, and go out to amuse themselves alone, they will be sure to accuse them of idleness and gossip on other days.

But, even after largely discounting the value of the answers, the fact remains that in ten cases out of fifteen the verdict was definitely given against the meetings. In one case it was vaguely favourable and in two vaguely unfavourable. In one, that of the housemaid, the meeting referred to was in the North of England, and was evidently a vigorous, self-supporting organization ; and in one the husband spoke quite enthusiastically. But the greater number condemned them unhesitatingly. The reason given at once, in nearly every case, was that they were centres of gossip ; the objection that members go for what they can get was generally given, but after a little more thought. It did not seem to be nearly so prominent in their minds.

If this in any way represents the general judgement of working people, surely the matter is extremely serious. The harm these organizations must be doing, if these judgements are at all fair, must be enormous. One hears of children being kept away from school in order that their mothers may go to the meeting, and telling untruths when questioned about it ; of ' mothers ' going to two, three, or even four meetings, a week ; that the more respectable women will not go to them ; and that the whole thing is a system of bribery between Church and Chapel. But still more serious is the fact that (as one can hardly doubt in the case) the Church is steadily ranging herself on the side of what (rightly or wrongly) goes against the conscience of the people. Public opinion is seldom altogether at fault, and even if the moral ideas of the masses are imperfect, and their judgements unfair, it is surely fatal to act in opposition to their ethical standards without even trying to find out what they are.

Several of those who answered said the idea of mothers' meetings was good enough, but that they were wrongly worked and that the wrong people went to them. Where they were well spoken of, either the members went to give and not to get, or there seems to have been some definite instruction given. Surely if they were always managed on these principles the whole scandal would vanish. The accusation of bribery would disappear ; the running about from one to another would be stopped ; if the women attending really learnt something, the meetings would be composed of the best type of mother ; the accusation of gossip would at least have less justification ; husbands would be glad for their wives to attend ; and religion would gain immensely in credit.

Would it not be possible for the unsatisfactory sharing-out savings-banks and the clothing clubs, bolstered up by bonuses, to be swept away, and for genuine principles of thrift to be taught at mothers' meetings ? Could not the reading of silly stories be got rid of, and the gatherings used to explain the work of the Registered Friendly Societies, to teach simple practical dressmaking, such as the paper-hanger's wife was taught, to give instruction in nursing, in the laws of health and feeding of children ? Could not occasional lectures be given on what is being done in the schools, to impress on the parents the importance of regu-larity, to try to induce them to keep their children at school after they are turned fourteen, to send them to evening classes ? Could not they be talked to on the different openings for their children, of service for their daughters, of the importance of their learning good trades ? Might not simple instruction in cookery be given ? Surely if this were done the mothers' meetings might in time become a valuable aid to social progress, and so, indirectly, to religion, instead of being a hindrance to both.[1]

[1] For further suggestions see *New Methods on the Mothers' Meeting.* Edited by E. Paget, with a preface by the Bishop of London. (Long-mans), 1915. 6*d.*

'LETTING PEOPLE ALONE'

' I beg—nay, command !—that you will not pounce.'—MRS. WILFER,
in *Our Mutual Friend*.

THE clergy are busy in church on Sunday mornings and evenings, and do not realize how the matter looks to those outside. The congregations within are small ; the masses perambulating the streets are vast. They are not exactly irreligious, but it never occurs to them to pass through the doors of the church. What is at fault ?

When by chance (I speak as a clergyman) you have to be in the streets at the hours of service the whole question looks quite different. I once passed down the main street of Southend on my way to a service at 11.15. The road was black with a stream of people coming from the station to the front. I felt that probably the great mass would have gladly spent half an hour in worship, that they would have been interested in seeing the churches of the town if they could have visited them with the same freedom that they could visit the concerts, the mission preachers, the Secularist orators, or the cinemas, but that they were not in the least likely to do so as things are now.

The other day I passed through the streets of London at 7 p.m. I saw at once that those frequent groups of father, mother, and baby were not likely to turn into any church unless they could wheel in the perambulator. But imagine the consternation of the sidesmen if they tried !—the getting it up the steps, the staring of the congregation, the manœuvring necessary in the narrow gangways, and the general fuss. No ordinary man could face it.

Newman, after his secession to Rome, once re-visited

M

St. Paul's. He describes his experiences in a letter to Dean Church :—

MY DEAR DEAN,

Yes, I was morally turned out on St. Stephen's Day, as I told you at that time. I did nothing but what you might have done at Chester or Carlisle, where you might not be known. I stood just inside the doors listening to the chanting, of which I am so fond. First came verger one, a respectable person, inquiring if I wanted a seat in the choir, half a mile off me. No, I said, I was content where I was. Then came a second, not respectful, with a voice of menace. I still said No. Then came a third. I don't recollect much about him, except that he said he could provide me with a seat. Then came No. 2 again, in a compulsory mood, on which I vanished. I am sure if I was a Dissenter, or, again, one of Mr. Bradlaugh's people, nothing would attract me more to the Church of England than to be allowed to stand at the door of a cathedral. Did not St. Augustine, while yet a Manichee, stand and watch St. Ambrose ? No verger turned him out. . . .

Ever yours affectionately,
J. H. NEWMAN.

Dean Church and his colleagues long ago altered this sad state of things at St. Paul's. It is now the one church where men go in and out freely and find pasture—though they are not yet allowed to take in the perambulator. But the old spirit is unchanged elsewhere. I went a few weeks ago to Evensong at a well-known London church. I was a little late and it was very full, so I slipped into the baptistery and stood against the wall to join in the Psalms. A churchwarden was strutting about in the body of the church. Presently he espied me and bore down on me. He waved his hand and said, ' There is a seat up there '. I said, ' Thank you, I'd rather stay here '. So he returned to his parade and continued his patrol during the rest of the service, except when he sat down for the prayers. Presently a verger came up and pointed to a chair and said (what was quite obvious), ' There is a seat there '. I am afraid I answered, ' You *should* learn to let people alone ', but I was irritated at having my worship so continually interrupted. He retired meekly, but kept his eye on me to return good for evil. When we came to the prayers and I knelt down, he saw his opportunity and reproachfully threw down a kneeler before me with an audible ' plop '. When the prayers were over he came up to me again and said, with a long-suffering air, ' *Now* would you like a seat ? ' The office was over, so I went out. A few Sundays after I was again passing by, and should have liked to have said my Evensong there, but I couldn't face all that again.

' The lesson of letting other people alone,' writes Dr. Fowler, in his *Progressive Morality*, ' is one which men are slow to learn, though there are few who in their own case do not resent any attack on their liberty of judgment or action.' Mr. Haweis tells us somewhere how a certain well-known member of the aristocracy came for several Sundays and sat in the gallery of his church till an officious verger went up to him and ' my lorded ' him, after which he never came again. Swift, Dr. Johnson tells us, ' went in London to early prayers lest he should be seen at church ', and how many people there are to-day who will come to an early service where they are let alone, but will not go at other times because they do not know who may not pounce down on them the moment they enter the doors. This is where the Roman Church has the advantage. She has brought to England the experience and tradition of foreign lands, where churches are large and the people are at home and move freely in them. It is not, I think, her discipline but her freedom that attracts.

Of course there are some people who like being descended upon. We see that elsewhere in life. There are certain cheap tailor shops where if you look in the window for a minute the proprietor sidles up to you and touts for orders. I suppose this pays with the class of customers that he caters for, or he would not do it, but most of us walk on at once. Or, if you go to Kew Gardens, and enter by the gate in the Green, you have to brave a running fire of tea-garden proprietors, who stand at their doors like spiders in their parlours, and shout at you a chant of the merits of their establishments. Most of us therefore prefer to enter the Gardens by Cumberland Gate. At shops or stores, where human nature is better understood and a larger and more educated class is catered for, you can go where you like and no one bothers you to buy, though the shopwalker is always there directly you want him. Why should not the Church be as wise in its generation as the children of this world ?

We want, then, to break down this bad tradition. We want first a number of people who will set about establishing a right of way in and out of church. We want a body of people who will insist on their rights to be let alone, to be allowed to stand and kneel when and where they please. We want men who, if they want to stand at the bottom of the church to listen to the sermon, will take the risk of having the preacher stop and call the attention of the whole congregation to them by saying : ' There's a seat up here in the front of the church '. They would probably not have to endure it more than once or twice. We want to train our children to come in and go out by themselves. We want, of course, to abolish pew rents and allotted pews. We want to work for clearing out unnecessary benches, for gaining space, freedom, spontaneity, and individuality of worship. The masses are accustomed to it elsewhere, at promenade concerts in the Queen's Hall, at open-air meetings in Hyde Park. We must accustom them to it in church too if the Church is to be the Church of the people.

RELIGION THE MOST EFFECTIVE INSTRUMENT IN EDUCATION

How charming is divine philosophy,
Not harsh and crabbed, as dull fools suppose,
But musical as is Apollo's lute.

MILTON, *Comus.*

ENGLISHMEN are becoming really interested in Education. It is being discussed in the Press. The values of science and of literature are being urged in rivalry. It is felt that our future, now, after the war will depend on our schools. The outlook is hopeful. The ' religious question ' is for the moment suspended.

But herein there is a danger. We may easily let the question of the place of religion in education drop out of our minds. If we do so we shall lose an instrument more effective for training the mind and imagination of the child than either science or literature can secure.

For the aim of a school is to guide. The master instructs, supervises, sets lessons, and arranges hours of study. He chooses the subjects talked and thought about, and selects the music and poetry to be learned. Still more is it his aim to surround the child with that which will continually and unconsciously carry him on along the way. The influence of the pictures on the walls, of the school building itself, of order, or quietness in movement and manner, of restraint and taste in dress and voice, of all that goes to make up the ' atmosphere ' of the school in which the child's life draws breath—these matter more than the curriculum. But these external influences, direct and indirect, are easily thrown off when the child goes outside. The best education is that which works from within outwards, which is active and self-created, since the child takes his self away with himself when he leaves school. So the good teacher aims continually at making the child learn to do things for himself, knowing that this is at once more immediately effective and more permanently lasting. The child's activities so begun in school, and in early years, will go on in the home, and continue all through his after-life.

On these two counts, as an effective instrument to train and guide, and as one that works from within, religion is the most effective instrument in education.

I.

The aim of education, in the narrow sense of schooling, is to teach the pupil to use his mind, just as the chief aim of games is to develop the body. Both have a further use in disciplining and forming the character, but I am now speaking rather of intellectual education than of moral and religious. This training of the mind, all agree, must be given in the school, while many would say that the other is a matter of the home and the church. The main instruments of intellectual exercise, beyond the preparatory arts of reading, writing, and arithmetic, are history, geography, and literature. For these the religious lesson offers a unique opportunity for carrying the mind back over the past, for broadening the outlook beyond the immediate present, and for seeing into the heart of things and giving them adequate and artistic expression.

The teaching of English History is apt to become hard and dull. The past of our nation has a complicated story. The difficulty of realizing other times is great, especially those in which civilization advanced and grew more complicated. Lest it should become a mere matter of dates and kings, as it did to Maria and Julia Bertram [1] (who, as the reader will remember, long before they reached the ages of twelve and thirteen could ' repeat the chronological order

---

[1] Jane Austen, *Mansfield Park*, ch. ii.

of the kings of England with the dates of their accession and most of the principal events of their reigns, as well as those of the Roman Emperors as low as Severus, besides a great deal of the heathen mythology, and all the metals, semi-metals, planets and distinguished philosophers '), the good teacher aims first at telling stories of things done in the past and of the lives of men, at showing how nations grew and present-day institutions developed, at giving a sense of reality to former times by visits to ancient buildings which have survived to the present day.[1]

Now, in the Old Testament we have such a history told in simple language, concerned with life lived under simple conditions in the childhood of the world, and, therefore, intelligible to the child, but under which lived men in situations which perpetually recur.   In the story of Pharaoh and the Israelites, of Jeroboam and Rehoboam, of Nebuchadnezzar and Daniel, we have illustrated the chief elements of political philosophy and the fundamental principles by which questions of labour troubles, constitutional government, or of the limits of the power of the State, can be decided.   In the Gospels we have a perfect biography by which ' truth embodied in a tale ' (a tale of perennial interest as the continued output of books and theories about Jesus of Nazareth abundantly testifies) may enter in at the lowly door of childhood.   In the Acts and in Church History we have the record of the growth from the beginning of an institution which has outlasted all other governments and is, to say the least, as near to the life of the child and as intelligible as the British Constitution.   Moreover, it may reasonably be hoped that the child who is not in most cases very likely to read any more English History (except in the making) after he has left school, will continue to study his Bible, or, at least, to hear it read in church.

Geography is apt to become a mere string of names

[1] See the Board of Education's *Suggestions for the Consideration of Teachers*, ch. viii, The Teaching of History.

learned by heart. Professor Findlay tells a story of a Scotch peasant boy who gave with complete accuracy all the capitals of Europe, and much impressed his hearers with his learning, till in reply to a further question, ' Is a capital a man or beast ? ' he answered without hesitation, ' It 's a beast '.[1] So the wise teacher begins with local geography, which he combines with Nature Study. He goes on with stories of adventure and descriptions of the customs of other lands. The meaning of a map is learned by drawing plans of the school and of the way home, by country excursions and by bicycle rides. Imagination is carried beyond the shores of England by Empire Day celebrations.[2]

Now in reading the Bible geography is incidentally learned. Not mere names of towns, but the influences of plains and hills, of rivers and desert, of Jordan and the Dead Sea, of the Lowlands and of the Nile, in shaping the fates of Jerusalem, Philistia, Babylon, Assyria, and Egypt. In learning his catechism (the substance, not the letter) the child gets a sense of local relationships, for his is a Church school, the Church is the Parish Church, a unit of the whole Church of England, the Cathedral is that of the Diocese, the Bishop comes for his confirmation. He gets a sense of the Holy Catholic Church dispersed throughout the world, for he says the creeds of Christendom, and worships with sacrament and prayers that bring him into touch not only with the past of Palestine, Greece, and Rome, but of all the countries where English speech is heard. He learns, too, to think of the masses outside, in India, China, and Africa, to help and pray for missions sent to them ; to contemplate. the chance that one day he may hear the call to go and take actual part in Church work overseas. And all this will, or at least may, go on unchanged after he has left school. All

---

[1] *Principles of Class Teaching* (Macmillan), 1911, p. 150. He seems to have had no apocalyptic intention, and the Scotch, it is said, do not make jokes.

[2] *Suggestions*, ch. vii, The Teaching of Geography.

through his life the same wider view will be put before him by the Church.

Much has been done for literature by the improvement of our reading books. More intelligent methods of learning to read are now adopted. Spelling (that training in unreason) is deferred till at least the sights and sounds of words are familiar. Dictation has practically been dropped. Much, too, is done to further the appreciation of poetry. Children learn to recite, to act Shakespeare.[1] Much is being done with music. We are bringing our children back to the national feeling that expressed itself in Folk Song. Really good music is accessible to teachers and is cheap—witness the publications of Messrs. Novello, Boosey, and Curwen,[2] and many others.

But no literature equals the literature of the English Bible, whose beauty, as Faber wrote, ' lives in the ear like a music that can never be forgotten, like the sound of church bells which the convert (to Romanism) scarcely knows how he can forgo ' ; none equals that of the Prayer Book since

> the souls of now two thousand years
> Have laid up here their toils and fears.[3]

And though our hymns leave much to be desired both in words and music, they furnish the poetry and music that count. They form the only effective rival for the mass of the people to the inanities and vulgarities of the music hall. With infinite pains we get up concerts, and succeed here and there in getting together choral societies and even musical festivals, but in every parish there is a choir that

[1] Cp. the English Association's Leaflets : No. 14, *The Early Stages in the Teaching of English* ; No. 21, *English Literature in Schools. Suggestions*, ch. iv, The Teaching of English.

[2] I have specially in mind Novello's *School Songs* series, Boosey's *Golden Treasury* series, and Curwen's *Folk Song, Graded, Premier*, and *Fellowship* song books.

[3] A. H. Clough, *Poems* (Clarendon Press), 1910, p. 68, ' Ah ! yet consider it again '.

sings each week (often very badly, no doubt), a congregation that meets with boundless opportunities for massed singing. And all this music and literature, the foundation of which is laid at school, will remain in the minds of men and women long after they have left school. The psalms will be chanted at weddings and funerals. The lessons will be read in church. Their one opportunity for most men of meeting with oratory, and of hearing the beauty of the English tongue not distorted by a provincial drawl or tainted with a Cockney twang, will be from the pulpit and the altar. All this will gather to itself associations of worth and beauty as the years go on, till even the paltry and mean will gain an inspiration of its own, while the deep and strong and noble will come ever nearer to an adequate expression of all that the hearts of men have learned by the experience of life, of life itself an education, we Christians believe, for another world.

It is surely, on the lowest grounds of mere intellectual and artistic education, sheer folly to try to cut out the religious lesson from the curriculum, and the religious influence from the school.

II

' An adequate expression of all that the hearts of men have learned.' Here is a further reason why religion is the most effective instrument in education. It works from within outwards, and not merely from outside.

Men may easily remain indifferent to the best surroundings. Peasants will live dull uninspired lives though surrounded by the finest scenery. There are failures from the best homes. Good government can only alter externals of life. ' How small,' wrote Dr. Johnson,

' of all that human hearts endure
That part which laws or Kings can cause or cure.'

And boys and girls have a wonderful power of remaining

impervious to all that is brought to bear on them from outside.

But a Church school makes religion a part of their lives. It teaches history because they live in it as members of a historic church, saying her traditional creeds, worshipping at her ancient altars, taking active part in her customs that survive from the past, adopting the imagery of ancient Palestine in speaking of Babylon, Jordan, and Zion, when thinking of life, death, and the world to come, chanting in her ancient modes, moving according to the rules of long established ceremonial. *Les cérémonies de l' Église plient à la politesse*,[1] wrote Joubert. Men gain thereby a continually growing sense of dignity such as that which is inherited by races of an older civilization. The more favoured members of English society show the effect of having been educated at the older universities and schools, but for every child of the whole people there lies at his door the like opportunity of learning to live as a unit of a body rich with the dower of a unique past.[2]

Christian life teaches geography from within, as gradually to the child experience of a greater world is written down in his heart. He is delivered from social narrowness by learning to worship with all classes. He sees strangers coming into

---

[1] *Pensées*, Titre I, cxii.

[2] 'As there is one mode of training for philosophers, another for orators, and another for athletes, so there is a generous disposition suitable to the choice that is set upon moral loveliness resulting from the training of Christ. And in the case of those who have been trained according to this influence, their gait in walking, their sitting at table, their food, their sleep, their going to bed, their regimen, and the rest of their mode of life acquire a superior dignity.'—Clement of Alexandria, *Paed.* I. xii.

So Dr. Illingworth. ' Finally, a sacramental religion has a natural influence on the manners. For by bringing our bodies into constant connexion with spiritual realities, it naturally affects their behaviour. And although this may seem to some a trivial thing to mention, it is not really so ; for behaviour has a more powerful reaction upon character than men often suppose.'—*Christian Character* (Macmillan), 1904, p. 165, ch. viii.

church, and kneeling by his side.   Their evident familiarity
with the forms of worship that he knows gives him a sense of
an unknown extension of the life he is living.   Insensibly he
borrows by imitation from others, and lives his life out into
theirs.   This stirs from within as he learns a sense of duty
to the congregation, as he takes his place in societies and
guilds, as he recognizes the badges of his organization worn
by strangers when he passes them in the street, as he learns
to pray for all.   I know no better training in sociology,
and none more practical, than to say the Litany in concert.
He gains a sense of social solidarity when, in travelling,
he finds the same service wherever he goes, a sense of
common worship when he feels that the cathedrals he visits
are the chief fanes of *his* Church.   The personal element
in this wider knowledge gives a reality and vigour to the
sense of world-citizenship with all the force and inner
intensity that religion alone can impart.

Again, it is not merely that in church he hears fine literature ;   he takes it to his lips and makes it his own.   He gains
a conception of nature from singing the Benedicite, that is,
at least, different and more impassioned than that given by
Nature Study.   He uses the words of the psalms and hymns,
and learns to speak in the language they provide.   This, too,
he does when most stimulated to appreciate their fullness of
meaning by the exaltation of sensibility wrought by sermons
and lessons, from the setting of architecture, the environment of music, and the companionship of men.   He learns to
take the words and phrases of the collects and use them,
not as things repeated by the echo of sounds impressed on
him from without, but as the spontaneous uprush of
the deepest thoughts and sincerest desires that spring
from the very centre of his being.   What more can Education do ?

III

We all of us know, do we not ? men and women who with no advantages of birth, have been made gentlemen and gentlewomen just by their Christianity and the inner refinement that it gives. This is what we want to secure for all. The ladder from the elementary school to the university that we hear so much about, can be climbed by very few, and those who scale it find themselves only too often at a height where they lose their heads, and can do nothing on the firm ground from which they came. At best they are but individuals out of the mass, and they lose much of their chance of helping that mass by leaving it. But the culture and breadth which religion gives, while it brings all classes together in one great democracy, strengthens natural ties and hallows them. It is in no way incompatible with simple lives or humble occupations. We cannot be satisfied with the present state of the democracy we know. Its vulgarity is witnessed by its songs, the narrowness of its interests is indicated by its amusements,[1] by its rudeness and its inarticulateness. I am not speaking of graver moral defects. I am not now arguing for the truth and worth of religion in itself. Simply as an instrument of mere school education we want to claim its aid as the one effective means of securing real breadth and refinement of mind for all the sons and daughters of the English nation and of the English Church.[2]

[1] We read that 30,000 men attended a football match a few years ago on Christmas morning.

[2] I have tried to work out the ideas contained in this paper, and others connected with Education, in my *Introduction to the Study of Pastoral Theology* (Oxford), 1912, Bk. III, ch. ii ; *Education and Pastoral Theology ;* and in my *Principles of Parish Work* (Longmans), 1905, ch. vii, ' Young and Old.'

INDEX

Printed in England at the Oxford University Press